December 2020

Lib,

To my cherished friend
and Wooster '66 Classmate.

Well, Penny & I didn't
make it to Union with you, Jim,
Gary & Marty because a voice
inside was suggesting I
seek another path. This book
is about that other path.

Penny joins me in wishing
you & your family the very best
in the years ahead. Much love,
Ken

Everybody In, Nobody Out

Inspiring Community at Michigan's
University Musical Society

KEN FISCHER WITH ROBIN LEA PYLE

FOREWORD BY WYNTON MARSALIS

University of Michigan Press
Ann Arbor

Copyright © 2020 by the University of Michigan

For questions or permissions, please contact um.press.perms@umich.edu

Published in the United States of America by
the University of Michigan Press
Manufactured in Canada
Printed on acid-free paper

First published August 2020

A CIP catalog record for this book is available from the British Library

ISBN 978-0-472-13202-7 (hardcover : alk. paper)
ISBN 978-0-472-12703-0 (ebook)

To my family for their enduring love and support . . .
In memory of Mom, Dad, and Jerry
With great appreciation to Norm and Martha
And immense gratitude to Penny, Matt, Renee, Alex, and Reid

Contents

Preface

During my years as president of the University Musical Society (UMS) at the University of Michigan (U-M), I was fortunate to have many opportunities to speak to groups about my experiences presenting the artists who visited our community. The groups especially liked the "backstage" stories, those that brought out the humanity of the musicians, actors, dancers, composers, and conductors. I spoke at service clubs and lifelong learning groups throughout the state; at University of Michigan alumni clubs in nearly every region of the country, including Camp Michigania in Northern Michigan and in the Adirondacks; and at U-M alumni travel programs that I hosted with my wife, Penny, throughout the world. I've continued to do these presentations since I retired from UMS on June 30, 2017.

After these presentations, people commented, "Get that story in print" or "You should write a book." I thanked them for their comments and thought to myself, "Yeah, someday." As retirement approached, and colleagues and friends asked about my plans, I found myself saying, "Maybe I'll write that book people have suggested."

Around the same time, I was visiting with prospective donors to the Victors for Michigan campaign, U-M's major fundraising initiative that had a goal of $4 billion (and when the campaign ended on December 31, 2018, U-M had raised $5.28 billion). Among the individuals I met with in the spring of 2016 were Tom and Debby McMullen, who had been supporting UMS concerts each year for the past two decades as corporate sponsors. Their love for the arts had deep roots: Tom was still playing his cornet, an instrument he'd studied in his youth with Roger Jacobi, an Ann Arbor Public School music educator and later Interlochen Center for the Arts president. He was looking forward to retirement.

I mentioned to Tom and Debby that, with Tom retiring, it might be a good time to take steps to assure that there would be an annual McMullen-sponsored performance each UMS season into the future. I also brought up my own impending retirement and that I was considering writing a book about my years at UMS. Tom and Debby were delighted to learn this and told me how much they'd enjoyed hearing me tell stories about the visiting artists over the years. One of my favorite stories actually involved Tom and local restaurateur Dennis Serras, who'd both played 18 holes of golf with Mikhail Baryshnikov when the dancer and actor was in Ann Arbor for a week doing a play for UMS in October 2004.

On May 13, Tom and Debby sent me a letter proposing a gift to UMS that would accomplish two objectives: first, to assure funding for a McMullen-sponsored concert each year for the next five years through the 2020–21 season; and second, to support my book project—to provide, in Tom's words, incentive for me to start it and finish it. The gift could be applied toward the purchase of books from the publisher, for editorial and promotional support, and for anything else that would help get the book completed. What a creative gift! And certainly one that any publisher would welcome. I had always intended that, if I did write a book about UMS, all proceeds would go directly to UMS to support its programs. The McMullens' gift would help guarantee healthy sales to propel that goal. It also meant to me that the book had better be good. The pressure was on!

One of my first challenges was to determine what the book would and would not be. It was easier to think about the latter. I didn't want to write a detailed history of UMS, or even just of the 30 seasons when I was at the helm. Comprehensively documenting the organization's history might be an interesting and valuable project for someone someday, but not for me. Nor did I want the book to be a "how-to" text on performing arts management. Having now taught several U-M courses in Arts Leadership, I know my experiences at UMS hold helpful illustrations of certain leadership and management principles and practices. And I did hope the book could offer something of value to both experienced executives and emerging professionals that they might apply to their work. At the same time, I was reluctant to force every story in the book to teach a lesson about leadership or management. Some stories are just good stories.

So what would the book be?

I wanted to write something for the UMS family, including our audiences, staff, volunteers, partners, and regional community. It needed to help them recall special performances and other events, to provide a sense of the inner workings of their organization, and to heighten their appreciation for the amazing team of dedicated professionals required to bring them the outstanding programs UMS presents year in and year out. I also wanted the book to offer something to the University of Michigan family of students, faculty, staff, alumni, and friends who might become more familiar not only with the oldest university arts presenter in the U.S. but also with a unit of their university that contributes significantly to our shared mission of teaching, research, and public engagement.

I decided the best way to achieve these aims was a chronological walk-through of my time with UMS, highlighting some of the memorable events, decisions, initiatives, and people experienced along the way. I would have to pick and choose the stories and necessarily leave some good ones on the cutting-room floor. The early part of the book would cover the 42 years of my life up to the point when I started the job at UMS on June 1, 1987, with a focus on the experiences that contributed to my eventual work in the arts. Throughout, I wanted to show how the path I took was guided by a philosophy that ultimately became this book's title. EINO—"Everybody In, Nobody Out"—was the inclusion policy of Washington, DC, impresario Patrick Hayes, founder of the Patrick Hayes Concert Bureau in 1947 and the nonprofit Washington Performing Arts Society in 1966. He was committed to desegregating the theaters of Washington and to assuring that the arts would be welcoming to all. During my years living in the DC area, Patrick became my good friend and mentor. Inspired by what "Everybody In, Nobody Out" accomplished in Washington, I brought EINO to UMS with Patrick's blessing, and it became our guiding light for my 30 years at UMS.

Even after determining the book's focus, I can't say writing was always easy. There were retirees who'd advised me, "Fisch, people will want you to do stuff, to take on leadership roles, join boards, after you retire. Say no to everything for a year." I didn't heed their advice and said yes to two invitations from people I couldn't say no to: Community leader Ismael Ahmed invited me to chair the new advisory board of Detroit's Concert of Colors diversity music festival, which he had founded 26 years before; and the King's Singers invited me to become president of their new King's Singers Global Foundation, an initiative the renowned British men's vocal ensemble created during their 50th anniversary year to support their commissioning, special projects, and charitable activities. I also taught my first collegiate-level course during the fall of 2017 for the School of Music, Theatre & Dance. Although only a one-credit, mini-course, it might as well have been a four-credit mega-course given the amount of time I spent developing and executing it. Those opportunities took time away from the book but brought great satisfaction.

When I did find time to write, I had assistance from two talented individuals. First, Robin Lea Pyle, who not only helped me organize, draft, and edit the manuscript in its early stages, but also provided constant encouragement along the way. Later Robin would read the final draft of the manuscript and offer valuable editorial suggestions. Second, Eric Engles, a developmental editor who helped me improve the structure and focus of the book. Eric was direct, confident, and persuasive, but always kind and understanding, taking the time to explain the recommendations he offered. He asked me many questions that demonstrated his deep investment in helping me make this a worthy book.

I'm told fact-checking is rarely an author's favorite part of writing a book. I loved it. The process of confirming numerous dates and details put me back in touch with artists, managers, teachers, administrators, camp counselors, close colleagues and friends, as well as UMS staff, board, and volunteer colleagues—all whom I had built relationships with over many decades. Renewing these relationships was a joyful experience for me, and I hope this comes through as you read the book.

A central role, both in completing this book and helping me through the events described within it, was played by my wife, Penny. She's been there the whole time providing encouragement. In fact, with my having met her at age 16 in the orchestra at Interlochen Arts Camp, Penny has known me 80% of my life. I couldn't have done this without Penny's constant love and support—and for her being the best possible first-line fact-checker with her great memory for detail. Thank you, Penny.

Foreword

by Wynton Marsalis

There have been many stories about the stresses and strains of touring. Long travel, bad food, missing family, the list goes on and on. Those things are unquestionably true, but there is another truth. Every performance, wherever you may be, is also a homecoming. And while the artist or star is the subject of commentary, criticism, and celebration, there are a handful of very basic, yet critical touch points to every concert that hold the keys to activating millions of connections.

These relationships are all conceived, facilitated, and executed by your presenter and their team. Acting as host, master of ceremonies, and conduit to the community, that team has labored over thousands of details—significant and trivial—to make a single concert a reality, and they do this again and again. It's God's work requiring the care of a first-time mother and the patience of a doting great-grandfather.

I have performed around the world for 40 continuous years and there is no finer team than the University Musical Society at the University of Michigan and no more dedicated a servant of the Arts and Culture than Ken Fischer. For me, he is the model, manifestation, and very definition of a great presenter.

Guided by a love of community, Ken's countless presentations have demonstrated not only respect for what his audiences wanted but a deeper commitment to what they needed. He possessed a belief in his own good taste and a very strong constitution to withstand democratic dialogue. Ken was and remains the definition of an arts rebel, fighting a guerrilla war from inside the establishment. He is, by necessity and by trade, a psychologist, chauffeur, salesman, gofer, psychiatrist, diplomat, educator, boss, cheerleader, businessman, lawyer, confidant, mentor, friend, disciplinarian, follower, financier, politician, raconteur, pollster, nurse, servant, and social worker. With a steady hand, he expertly navigates all of these roles and deftly fields the countless number of things that can and do go wrong. On top of it all, he has nerves of steel because . . . the show must go on.

I am so proud to be his most presented artist: 19 times in 30 years. I only wish there were more. I first got to know Ken in 1996, when UMS presented the Lincoln Center Jazz Orchestra Octet for the first time at the Michigan Theater. A year later, we came back with my oratorio, *Blood on the Fields,* in Hill Auditorium, and a year after that with a program that combined Stravinsky's *L'Histoire du soldat* with the world premiere of my own composition, *A Fiddler's Tale*, in Rackham Auditorium. A couple of years later, we performed a Swing Dance party at the Eastern Michigan University Convocation Center.

In a period of five years, Ken presented our group five times in four different venues and in very different contexts. Though we have played in many venues, I will focus on Hill Auditorium, where most of our concerts took place.

It's a large house and not always easy to fill. But time and time again, Ken kept it packed with the most diverse listening community that exists anywhere in these United States. With UMS, you would see a college arts series with actual students in attendance. In almost all colleges, Arts were for alumni and teachers, and entertainment and spectacle were for students. Here . . . students overflowed because Ken was out there recruiting them to the cause.

UMS audiences have experienced a startling array of musical styles, artists, and world-class ensembles, new commissions, and innovative presentations. They feel at home and free to be themselves, expressive and unbridled in their response to sublime moments. When you sound great, they are with you; when you struggle, they carry you. If you are lucky enough to play for them, "you feel them." And Ken was out there cheering with the best of 'em.

Let me take you through a composite day at Hill with Ken, one that has become 'second nature' across these decades.

It all begins with a *'journey'*—be it by plane, car, boat, or all of the above. The organization and particulars of this trip is the first indication of the class, clarity, and concern of your presenting hosts. When you arrive, Ken is there to welcome you.

Your travel takes you to a *'home,'* Hill Auditorium. Upon arrival, you get an immediate and visceral feeling. There is a presence and an energy permeating the rooms and corridors. A living history speaks from the photos and posters on the walls, to the creaks and cracks of the stage floor and out past the proscenium into the resonant body of the room. Ken is there watching you figure things out.

Your formal introduction is called a 'soundcheck.' Here you meet the stage crew and assess their disposition, as well as the ambience and guts of the room. The crew can, many times, be at odds with the management. Here, all is aglow and you're happy. After the soundcheck, in the silence and loneliness of an empty hall, you can hear the whispering ghosts of past performances. If you are quiet enough, you can channel the nervous anticipation of past performers and hear the cheers of triumphant nights forever gone, the murmurs of tepid receptions and the deafening silence of abject failures.

After the soundcheck you are served a '*meal*' that teaches you about more than just the popular chicken dish of the region. How and where it is laid out and by whose hands, let alone the quality, reveals and reiterates the care and concern of your presenting hosts. Ken is in there with you eating and joking and clowning, and you are "at home" on the road.

Then the 'concert' itself. After Ken delivers some gracious, inspiring, and welcoming words, the audience is warmed up; you are up over wires onto a battleground to play away the blues of everyday life for a group of strangers, who are soon to become 'one' in pursuit of an elusive, but palpable mutual happiness. It is the ritual recreation of an event as ancient as storytelling. That concert remembers *and* foretells for artist and audience alike, what has meaning *to* us and what it means to *be* us. How that audience looks and feels, how it listens and responds, and how it discerns and assesses, is the heart of the matter. And, *that* tells you all you really need to know about the substance of your presenter's aspirations.

The '*post-concert reception*' immediately follows. It's for sponsors and supporters, and here you meet the intricate network of sophisticated citizens who bring noncommercial art to this community. This gathering tops off the evening and must be handled gracefully and graciously and timed just right. The aspirations and dreams in this room will most likely become future cultural achievements for us all. Ken and Penny are there. And, he is the master of hosting, cajoling, reminding, leading, and following, very much on duty, piloting the room to ensure everyone had a good time, everything was right, and that future calls to duty would be eagerly affirmed.

After some photos, anecdotal exchanges, and critical 'fare-thee-wells', we are off to a *'meet-and-greet'* with dedicated fans, students, and friends who have patiently yet still eagerly waited on what can feel like the end of a very long receiving line. Before you are a class of kids, old friends, and cousins (you didn't know you had). You see fans of all ages and persuasions and, as the night goes on, you notice that Ken is still amongst them, still hanging in. You sign and talk to people and listen to kids play and happily receive some homemade oatmeal cookies and maybe a pound cake. This has been a long day. Whew . . .

And you realize at this point in the night, that over the years, Ken is there. And he is a man whose presence *is* friendship. And his achievement can't be assessed in grand terms over the broad canvas of years. Because for him, every night, every performance was the most important thing that has ever happened. That is why he was always there.

Ken understood that for the concertgoer: it is your first night out with your 8-year-old daughter or son to see some piece they may fall asleep on, but refer to as a touchstone forever; it is your 89-year-old grandmother's favorite artist and you've gotten the same seats she sat in with your grandfather for 65 years on her first night out after he has passed away; it is your 19-year-old's hope to initiate a group of underprivileged and deprived middle-school kids in the wonders of a long form composition; it is the only chance you will ever have to see something you have waited your entire life to see, and it is right before you, be it from Russia or Pakistan or Louisville, Los Angeles or London. And when you leave that concert . . . your life is never the same, because something that was only a distant dream has come to you, in Ann Arbor.

It is the expansion of consciousness and it is the great coming together around something of substance and meaning. Ultimately, it is the essence of what we can give to one another, an enriching human experience that becomes an indelible landmark on the panorama of our lives.

And for Ken, each night has been the culmination of years and years of asking: asking managers if their artists are available, negotiating fees, asking for breaks on travel and hotels and asking for catering, asking for time and space in the hall, asking teachers and students to attend something they may not be familiar with, asking donors and alumni and sponsors to support performances at different levels, asking stage crews to wait a little longer to close the hall, asking drivers for a little more time, asking artists to talk to supporters and fans and students, and asking Penny and

Matt and family to be with him and to wait and wait and wait. And, asking them to be with you, to come with you and be hospitable, to be kind and be giving of time and energy, night after night, deep into the night. Asking and more asking.

And at the very end of a long day and night, many times across 30 years, he's looking at me trying to see if I want to go, and I'm saying "no man I'll talk to everyone," and he's saying "we have to close the hall," and I'm waving him off, and he's trying to make sure everything is cool, saying to everyone, "It's been a long day folks," and I'm talking to the last of the students and listening to them play, and it's now well past the hour he should be home and the hall should be closed . . . but here we are. Me and him. And it's past midnight when we get into the car and he says, "How are you doing? You want to go get something to eat and talk about things?" And I laugh and look at him and we both start laughing.

It's now 3 a.m. and the band is back on the road and I'm saying to myself, "Ain't but one thing makes somebody do all of the things he did night in and night out." Belief. And it's all up in this book.

one
Music at the Heart

Music was an inescapable part of my childhood. My parents, Beth and Gerald Fischer, believed that learning to play an instrument and singing and playing with others were good for developing discipline and self-esteem—not to mention bringing great personal satisfaction—and so those activities were mapped out for me from the beginning. Dad, who had paid for his education at Rutgers in part by playing the piano for the Rutgers Glee Club, wanted all his children to know the piano. My mother agreed, and it was decided that we would all begin piano lessons in second grade. My older brother Jerry embarked on his lessons in 1951, when I was seven years old.

By this time my family, which consisted of younger brother Norman in addition to Jerry and me, had moved from Washington, D.C., to Plymouth, Michigan, a suburb of Detroit. In addition to being a great place to grow up, Plymouth had cultural amenities that included the Plymouth Symphony Orchestra (now known as the Michigan Philharmonic). My father joined the board of directors of the orchestra, eventually becoming its president, and both he and Mom sang in the First Presbyterian Church choir.

In the summer of 1954 Jerry was old enough to attend National Music Camp at Interlochen in northwest lower Michigan, about a four-hour drive from Plymouth. My parents had high regard for the camp's founder, Dr. Joseph E. Maddy, and talked about the camp as an ideal place to spend the summer. They made it clear to all three of us that attending Interlochen, as it was informally known, would be a joy and privilege. Though I had started my piano lessons, my parents didn't think I was quite ready for the rigor of National Music Camp. They sent me instead to a recreational camp called Haza Witka not far from Interlochen. I enjoyed the traditional program of riflery, archery, and such and looked forward to the prospect of a music-filled summer the following year.

In fourth grade at Bird Elementary School in Plymouth I made friends with Chuck Ellis. At a school-sponsored family potluck meal, Chuck and I arranged for our families to sit next to each other. In no time, my dad discovered that Chuck's mom Jean played cello and his dad Charlie played violin. Next thing we knew, our parents decided to devote every Thursday night to playing trios for piano, cello, and violin, at our house one week and at the Ellises' the next. When the soirée occurred at our house, my brothers and I would to go to bed listening to the wonderful chamber music.

With this exposure to an ensemble, it was only natural for us to gravitate toward instruments other than piano. Jerry began playing the clarinet, Norman the cello and trombone. I began playing cornet. Only too happy to facilitate our development as musicians, our parents started driving us to Ann Arbor for private lessons from professors at the University of Michigan's School of Music.

That drive from Plymouth to Ann Arbor was always a wonderful trip to make on Saturday mornings. We would take Geddes Road to pass by the home of Dr. Maddy in hopes of catching a glimpse of the man who, in 1928, had founded the institution that would play such a prominent role in our lives. We loved going to Ann Arbor and we'd often stay for the football games.

In the summer of 1955 it was my turn to be initiated into the eight-week-long National Music Camp experience. I was 10 years old, ready to broaden my horizons, be away from home again, and immerse myself in music. When I arrived at the idyllic natural setting of Interlochen, I met my two counselors, Lynn Doherty and Lee Cabutti, and clicked with them immediately. Both were athletes and coaches and would show themselves to be excellent mentors.

During that summer I took a course in Music Talent Exploration, where each week we were exposed to a different instrument. I played the harp, drums, saxophone, and flute, among others. In the seventh week, the teacher, Dr. Arthur Williams, knowing my principal instrument was cornet, encouraged me to try the French horn. He pointed out how much more versatile the horn was and how there was always a need for horn players. I played horn for the next two weeks, and it started to take hold of me.

At Interlochen, I loved being surrounded by people who, like the members of my family, shared a deep love of music and all the arts. Since the students who came to camp to study were from all over the globe, my eyes were opened to the great diversity of languages and cultures in the world. And I could see that despite our outward differences the universal language of music brought us together in common cause.

One of my important achievements that summer had nothing to do with music. All the boys in Cabin 7 except me had swum the one mile across Duck Lake. Even though I had just learned to swim and was intimidated by the distance, I didn't want to be the only one not to have performed the feat. Encouraged by Lynn and Lee, I decided to give it a try. With camp swim coach Gus Stager—who was also the swimming coach at the University of Michigan and would soon be named the coach of the U.S. Olympic swim team—encouraging me and with Lynn rowing beside me in a boat and offering support, I made it across the lake safely. Afterwards, it felt like anything was possible.

Though I couldn't attend Interlochen the following summer because of a three-week family road trip through Colorado, Arizona, and Utah, I returned in 1957 for what would be the first of two summers in the Intermediate Boys camp.

After dinner one evening in April 1957, my parents called a family council and announced that we would soon have an addition to the family. "Are we getting a dog?," asked Norman excitedly. "An exchange student?," suggested Jerry. I surmised that the formal occasion entailed something more serious and speculated that we were adopting a new sibling. None of us could imagine that our 41-year-old mother was pregnant. But that was the astounding news delivered by our parents.

We tracked Mom's expanding belly with anticipation. Though a hospital birth was planned, Mom went into labor unexpectedly in the early morning of December 7. Delivery began before the ambulance arrived, and both Dad and I helped bring a baby girl into the world. She was christened Martha Anne. Old enough to participate meaningfully in her care, we boys were taught how to change Martha's diapers and give her a bottle and a bath. It made us feel very grown up, especially when Mom explained that these skills would serve us well when we had our own families.

The Fischer family in the early 1960s: clockwise from left: father Gerald J. Fischer, Kenneth (b. 1944), Norman (1949), Gerald B. (1943), Martha (1957), and mother Beth Buckley Fischer.

Once I reached high school, the sessions at Interlochen became more serious, though no less satisfying. For three summers in the orchestra program—first, in 1960, as a member of the concert orchestra and then in the National High School Orchestra in 1961 and 1962—I learned and performed one symphony a week. This meant that by the end of each summer I had become intimately familiar with the French horn parts for eight different symphonies. Each summer, we also sight-read other symphonic works, played overtures and tone poems, and in the high school and festival choirs we sang many of the great oratorios. For a couple of years I was also in the high school band. Every week, I performed in orchestra, in band, and in choir. And if that wasn't enough, we rehearsed and performed a Gilbert and Sullivan operetta each summer. (I had leads in two of the three operettas I performed in, including the role of Lord Mountararat in *Iolanthe*.) During these three summers, I was rehearsing or performing all the time, learning an immense volume of repertoire and getting exposed to many of the great composers. It was hard work, and great fun.

Though the Interlochen program recognized that not all of us would go on to have careers as professional musicians, it incorporated competition as both preparation for a musical career and an incentive for preparation and practice. Members of both the band and the orchestra took part in weekly "challenges." When you first arrived at the beginning of the summer you'd be assigned a specific chair to occupy (within your instrument's section) based on how well you'd played in the opening audition, with the first chair being held by the highest-ranked musician. At the end of each week thereafter, if you wanted to advance your position, you could challenge the person ahead of you. The instructor would select a solo or other passage in a section of a piece for the two of you to play in sequence. Those in the rest of the ensemble would put their heads down to listen and then vote on who performed best.

When I returned to Interlochen in 1961, I didn't think my audition went very well. When I checked the roster, however, my name was at the top of the French horn list. I went to see horn teacher Marvin Howe, who had auditioned me, asking how I could have placed first with what I thought was a mediocre audition. He agreed that it "wasn't a stellar audition," but explained his reasoning: "You're a good guy, you've been around here for a long time, and you know the ropes, and you know where the music goes. When the challenges come up at the end of this week you'll find your rightful spot." It felt good to have Mr. Howe's trust, but his last point sounded a little ominous. As it turned out, we were playing Sibelius's Second Symphony that first week. I'd been rehearsing it the entire previous year, sitting in the first horn spot with the Michigan Youth Symphony. So I had the score down cold and was able to keep my first chair for the first four weeks. And though I lost first chair during challenges in the fifth and sixth weeks, I regained it for the final two weeks.

Being first-chair French horn in the final week meant something very special. It was a beloved tradition at Interlochen for a camp-wide orchestra, chorus, and dance corps to perform Liszt's tone poem *Les Preludes* on the closing day of the season. Every instrumentalist, chorus member, and dancer from the Intermediate Division on up could participate. Dr. Maddy had established this tradition because he wanted every student to think of his or her National Music Camp experience as the "prelude" to a new life. The conclusion of *Les Preludes*, when the dancers come out and everyone is playing, was guaranteed to bring tears. For the performance closing out that summer, I got to play the beautiful horn solos in both Brahms's First Symphony and in *Les Preludes*.

Ken and Penny in
July 1971 at 'their
tree' at Interlochen
Arts Camp where
they met in 1961.

During the first week of that summer, while playing in the orchestra, I couldn't help but notice the attractive blonde flute player who was sitting a few rows in front of me. I got into cahoots with her stand partner so that I would be the one who would hand her the music she needed to rehearse. We met at the end of the first week and I learned that her name was Penny Peterson. After the usual chitchat, I asked her if she'd like to join me for the concert that evening. She informed me she already had a date. Undeterred, I asked, "how about tomorrow night?," and she accepted. I don't remember the details of that evening, but I did learn that Penny was from Mason City, Iowa, the hometown of flutist and composer Meredith Willson, who wrote *The Music Man* and modeled the musical's River City on his hometown. I was impressed that Penny not only knew Willson but had actually performed with him as a young girl.

We went together all summer. Although we were both busy with our respective rehearsals and performances, it's likely that others saw us as inseparable. At the end of the summer, we had a teary good-bye. Our initial separation would be short-lived, however. Penny's dad was attending a conference in Chicago only a week later and she could easily tag along. My family had met Penny and liked her and her family very much, so when I asked if we might all hop in the car and spend the weekend in Chicago so that I might have a chance to see Penny again, my parents and siblings were all in.

Penny and I agreed to meet on the steps of the Field Museum at 1:00 p.m. My family and I were delayed in getting into Chicago, however, and I had to race to the museum upon our arrival in order not to be late. I arrived at the bottom of the large set of steps right on time and saw Penny waiting for me at the top. It was the first time I had seen her in a dress, since the camp uniform was knickers all the time. She looked fabulous. I ascended the steps as she descended, and we had a warm embrace right in the middle. Our courtship continued thereafter through letters and occasional visits.

Having had success in the horn section in the summer of 1961, I decided to come back for a final summer at Interlochen in 1962 even though I had graduated from high school and decided that I didn't have the chops and dedication to become a professional musician. Dr. Maddy had announced at the end of the 1961 season that President Kennedy had invited Interlochen to bring its high school orchestra and dancers to the White House for a performance on the lawn the following summer, and I wanted to be there.

At the opening audition that summer, however, some younger kids cleaned my clock. Though they were sophomores and juniors in high school, they were much better than I was. I knew I had my work cut out for me if I was going to go to the White House. The day of the White House orchestra audition my position fell from fourth chair to sixth chair, and only the top five horn players would be going. I was devastated.

I decided to focus my attention on operetta, where I had secured a lead role, and to celebrate the success of my five colleagues going to the White House. Three days before the orchestra was to leave for Washington an astonishing announcement was made. Three instrumentalists were being added to the 100-member orchestra—one violin, one trumpet, and one French horn. I would get to go after all!

The entire experience was very special. We did a warm-up concert on August 5, 1962 on the grounds of Henry Ford's Fairlane Estate on the

U-M Dearborn campus before flying to the Washington area, where we stayed overnight at Fort Belvoir in northern Virginia. The next morning we went to the lawn of the White House. As we were seated on the stage and getting ready to play, in flew the helicopter with President Kennedy on it. He came to the stage and, using no notes, addressed the audience for four spell-binding minutes, talking about why symphony orchestras are important for America. He talked about kids training in music and how much discipline was involved. I'll never forget how he said that more people go to symphony concerts than to baseball games, and that both are good for America. After the speech, he turned around to address the orchestra, telling us he was going to go to the Oval Office to do some work but he'd keep all the doors and windows open so he could hear us.

We played our hearts out. After the concert was over the president had us gather in the Rose Garden and then invited us for lunch inside. We picked up a buffet lunch in the State Dining Room and walked to the East Room. I sat on the room's wood parquet floor with Peggy Rusk, the daughter of Secretary of State Dean Rusk, on my right, and Kathy McNamara, the daughter of Secretary of Defense Robert McNamara, on my left. The children of cabinet officials were our hosts for the day, and Peggy and Kathy were about my age. The next day, on the front page of the *New York Times*, there was a photograph of the dancers and President Kennedy, with the White House in the background. What a wonderful opportunity it was for us to be in his presence and to have him welcome us so warmly to the White House.

Later that day we went sightseeing. Since I was born in Washington and had visited the city many times, I didn't need to do everything the other kids were doing. When they were visiting the Jefferson Memorial, I decided just to relax and lay down on a seat toward the back of the bus. Joseph Maddy, the revered founder of Interlochen and our conductor, came in and sat in the front of the bus, not thinking anyone was there. In his excitement over what the day had held, he started talking to himself loudly enough for me to overhear him. "This is Washington, this is the beginning," I heard him say. "What is next? We can do more of this." I never acknowledged that I was there, but this genius who made things happen by the sheer force of his will continued to voice his dreams.

In the autumn of 1962, I enrolled at The College of Wooster in Ohio, as my brother Jerry had done the year before. (It wasn't the first time I had followed Jerry's lead, and it wouldn't be the last.) Mine was the "Centennial Class" because we would graduate in 1966, the 100th anniversary of the college. In describing us during orientation week, a college official said we were not so much "well rounded" as we were "elliptical." None of us quite knew what he meant, but we assumed it indicated a special status—something we all tried to live up to. I dabbled in a variety of subjects that year, and especially enjoyed French with Frances Guille. I also found time to sing in the choir, play horn in the orchestra, join the track team, and pledge Third Section, a local fraternity.

After that first year of college, I wanted to spend the summer making some good money. My father, an executive with Ford Motor Company, offered to help me find an office job for the summer. I decided instead to take my chances with what would be a higher-paying job. I joined the United Auto Workers union, got in the line at the Rouge factory complex in Dearborn, and was assigned to the Frame Plant's "Hell Hole," so named because it was a physically demanding, noisy, and dirty place.

I found myself working on a line with 15 men. I was the only white person on the line and the youngest. Five of us had the task of meshing the side rails of an automobile frame together with chisels and sledgehammers while the line was moving; after we were done with it the frame would move into a tunnel where welders would weld the two sections of the frame together. Each part of the side rail was lifted off a moving line above the floor by two very large, muscular men who would then throw the side rail onto the mold while the line was moving. The five of us would spend 20 seconds beating the two side parts together, and then have about 10 seconds off before the next two sections would come by, needing to be meshed together.

I learned quickly that a way to get along with my coworkers on the line was to show interest in their lives. Most had children and were working hard to provide greater opportunities for them than they had had. In the 10 seconds or so we had between beating the side rails of one frame together, I could lean over the line where the side rails traveled and yell into the ears of my fellow worker—we wore earplugs and helmets—asking about his family. Since we could exchange words for only a few seconds out of every minute, a conversation that might take us 20 minutes under normal circumstances could take up to two hours on the line. In this way I earned my coworkers' respect and overcame my own fear of being excluded because I was different.

One day, I joined a group of the welders for lunch, each with our lunch pails. I sat next to one gentleman who was at least as old as my father and learned his first name was John. I asked him about his family. When he said "I have a son who plays the violin," I immediately flashed on the face of the only African American violinist I knew, a man named Darwyn Apple who had been the concertmaster of the Interlochen orchestra two summers previously. I leaped up and asked, "Are you the father of the great violinist Darwyn Apple?" John, astonished at my reaction, said yes. He couldn't believe that one of the workers on his line had been in the same orchestra as his son. John Apple took me straight away to his locker, where out fell magazine and newspaper articles about his son. One profiled Darwyn as the only black member of the Eastman Philharmonia on its trip to Western Europe, the Middle East, and the Soviet Union. The unlikely coincidence of meeting Darwyn Apple's father on an auto assembly line gave me a profound appreciation for how race and class all too often create artificial separations that deprive us of essential human connection.

Following my summer job in the factory, I returned to The College of Wooster for my second year, preparing to become a religion major. I enjoyed performing in the college choir and orchestra and took horn and voice lessons for credit, continuing on the path of being a competent amateur musician, content with making a worthy contribution to any ensemble of which I was a member. Penny, in contrast, was majoring in flute performance at the University of Iowa, sights set on a professional music career. We saw each other as often as we could, falling in and out of love with each other and with other people.

To give our long-distance relationship the time we felt it deserved, we both enrolled in summer school at the University of Iowa in 1964 after our sophomore year. We lived in homes adjacent to one another, took some of the same classes, sang in the same church choir, and enjoyed nearly every meal together. We concluded that this was a relationship that could really stick and committed ourselves to seeing it through despite the distance separating us during the school year.

In the fall of my senior year at Wooster I met William Sloane Coffin Jr., the chaplain at Yale University. I was deeply inspired by him; he was a preacher, counselor, intellectual, and social activist, in addition to being a compassionate human being who could tell stories, enjoy a beer, speak five languages, and play one heck of a piano. A major figure in the antiwar movement, he was challenging college students in the country to search their conscience and think critically about the war in Vietnam.

A group I was involved with, the Campus Christian Association at Wooster, had invited Coffin to our campus for four days in the fall of 1965. I was his principal host and rarely left his side. I had been planning to become a campus minister so spending a week with the Yale chaplain would be an extraordinary opportunity. While he was at Wooster I studied his every move; I watched his preaching, observed him always making time for students, and saw his authenticity and adept intellect in play when he engaged with people. He could take on any question and respond cleverly. I hadn't understood the full range of abilities required of a highly effective college chaplain until I observed them with Coffin. I concluded, with some disappointment, that I didn't have what I would need to have to be as effective as he was. While Coffin caused me to question my career direction, he also inspired me to move out of my comfort zone and work more actively for justice and peace.

After Coffin left Wooster and I continued to contemplate my future, the prospect of being a college chaplain or even a conventional pastor seemed a diminishing prospect. When I looked in the mirror, I would question whether the ministry was right for me. I knew there were other things that I could do, so I began to ponder what else I could do on a college campus that had value.

While I was at Wooster I had been invited to become a Rhodes Scholar candidate. In the essay I had written as part of the process, I had described myself as an "enabler," a person who makes things happen himself or inspires others to do so. Though I wasn't advanced beyond the state level in the Rhodes Scholar competition, I remembered very clearly that moment of self-awareness in which I self-identified as an enabler. Perhaps, I thought, I was on the way toward connecting people as my life's work.

Graduating from Wooster at the end of my senior year in 1966, I was as concerned with another major life issue—relationship—as I was with career. Penny and I had ultimately sustained our relationship through the course of our undergraduate studies, and we still felt very much in love. We decided to get married and tied the knot on July 2, 1966. Having secured jobs at Interlochen, that's where we went for the summer. I was the camp's director of transportation and Penny worked as a secretary for track coach Kenneth Doherty, typing the manuscript for the second edition of his classic *Modern Track and Field*.

The question of what do next proved very distracting. One week I was thinking that maybe I would be a doctor, the next week, a lawyer or a teacher. I had been admitted to Union Theological Seminary in New

York City, a progressive institution affiliated with Columbia University, and my two best friends from college, Gary Brown and Jim O'Brien, were going there. Moreover, Penny had planned to go to Juilliard, which was across the street from Union Theological Seminary (Julliard didn't move to its current location until 1969). I decided, however, that I had to do something else. At the same time, the war was breathing down my neck. Healthy American males in 1966 had three choices: Canada, Vietnam, or graduate school. I didn't want to serve in a war I didn't believe in, but I was not about to burn my draft card and move to Canada either. It seemed that graduate school was the best option.

We decided we would move to Ann Arbor. In some ways it was a desperate decision; it was close to the end of the summer and we hadn't made up our minds about what we were going to do in the fall. But in other ways it made perfect sense. My parents lived in Plymouth, about 17 miles away from Ann Arbor. I was a Michigan resident, and could go to school at the University of Michigan with in-state tuition; Penny was also a Michigan resident because she had married me. But for me the question loomed: What graduate program to apply to?

Having written a paper in my senior year at Wooster on the role of church-related colleges, I started thinking about becoming an administrator on a college campus. I discovered, thumbing through the U-M catalog—I was that desperate—that there was a program in the study of higher education. Penny and I came down to Ann Arbor on my day off from Interlochen and talked with John Brubacher, interim director of the Center for the Study of Higher Education. We liked what we heard. I applied for admission and soon after was accepted to the program. We moved to Ann Arbor right after the end of my job at Interlochen.

To help us afford my graduate school expenses, Penny got a job working as assistant to Gail Rector, the president of the University Musical Society. I began my program with enthusiasm, but feeling a little out of my league. Most of the other people entering the program that year had experience working in the world of higher education. At 21, I was the youngest, and the next youngest, 26-year-old Ted Marchese, had a law degree from Georgetown and had worked for the American Council on Education. Another cohort member, 27-year-old Marvin Peterson, had received his MBA and been an assistant dean at Harvard Business School. All were highly talented and ambitious. I felt incredibly lucky to be hanging out with these bright, experienced, and engaged people. They welcomed me

Ken's two predecessors at UMS and terms of service as president. From left: Charles A. Sink (1927–57); Sink's wife, Alva Gordon Sink; and Gail W. Rector (1957–87).

to their after-class coffee gatherings at the Brown Jug and to their lunches in the "Corner House."

Most of them would finish their coursework and prelims in two years and then be involved in their dissertation research. It would take me four years to get my coursework and my preliminary examination done.

During that time—the years 1966 through 1970—intensifying opposition to America's involvement in the Vietnam War was generating such serious unrest and conflict that everyone felt on edge. Penny and I didn't get directly involved in protests at first, but we did feel a need to be politically active. In 1968 I was one of more than a thousand University of Michigan students who got out of our jeans and sweatshirts and put on coats and ties and dresses to go to Milwaukee, where we canvassed voters for Sen. Eugene McCarthy right before the Wisconsin primary. It was called the "Clean for Gene" campaign. There were so many Michigan students participating that we were able to visit every single home in South Milwaukee.

In the meantime, I maintained connections to the world of musical performance through Penny. During the two years Penny was Gail Rector's assistant, I helped out by driving such artists as Mstislav Rostropovich, Andres Segovia, Ezio Flagello, and Mildred Miller to and from the Detroit airport. In 1967, during my second year as a graduate student, Gail asked us to pick up Mstislav Rostropovich at the airport, following the May Festival concert where Rostropovich's wife, Galina Vishnevskaya, and Mildred Miller were performing. Rostropovich himself would be performing the next afternoon. When the concert was over, Penny and I went to get the renowned cellist, who was arriving on a late flight. We owned an old Ford wagon with its share of rust on it, so we borrowed my father's Mercury. We waited at the airport gate area and watched everyone disembark. We didn't see anyone else. We were about to leave when a gentleman appeared with a cello. It was Rostropovich. We'd heard he had an ebullient character and liked to give big hugs, and we were hoping we might get one even though we were strangers. We approached him and identified ourselves as from UMS. He put his cello down in front of him, blocking any chance for an embrace or even a handshake. He looked at us and said, "Before we greet, I have a question. Did my wife get a standing ovation tonight or not?" Penny and I looked at each other and I said, "Mr. Rostropovich, you must understand that the people of Ann Arbor just don't stand. . . ." Before I could finish explaining that standing ovations were rare, he persisted, "Did she, or didn't she?" I said, "Well, two people stood." He asked who they were, and Penny said, "Her manager and her publicist." He smiled. "Tomorrow afternoon, I play Dvorak concerto. Guess who will get a standing ovation?"

During graduate school I also continued to play and perform music for fun. I founded a brass sextet called the Goliard Brass Ensemble, named after a band of roving students in 12th- and 13th-century Europe known for rioting and intemperance. Brass ensemble music had been a love of mine since I began playing in the brass choir at Interlochen in 1957 and I couldn't imagine anything more satisfying to do when I wasn't reading and studying.

After 1968, with the civil rights movement and opposition to the war roiling American society, Penny and I decided it was time to put ourselves on the line, in the spirit of William Sloane Coffin Jr. In October 1969, we rode a bus from Ann Arbor to Washington, D.C., to join 500,000 others for the National Moratorium Against the War in Vietnam.

Then, on May 4, 1970, four Kent State students were shot and killed by their contemporaries from the National Guard. Ten days later was the tragedy at Jackson State, where police fired on a group of students, killing two and injuring 12. It seemed we were in the midst of a horrible crisis: young people were being killed by their peers as they exercised their rights of free speech. And it hit very close to home because the Kent State students had been protesting the war, just as Penny and I and so many others had been doing at the University of Michigan. At Jackson State, a predominantly black college in Mississippi, the violence erupted due to rising tensions between the students, local youths, and law enforcement. It was a difficult, turbulent time to be a student on a college campus.

By June 1970 I'd finished my preliminary doctoral work and had only to begin and complete my dissertation. Penny had completed a master's degree in music and was preparing to enter a doctoral program in contemporary performance. I was getting tired of graduate school, so we decided to take a break and house-sit for my parents in Connecticut, where they had recently moved. We were watching television on a Friday night when the *Huntley-Brinkley Report* came on NBC and announced that President Nixon was forming the President's Commission on Campus Unrest to look at the issues of violence on college campuses. He wanted a report on his desk before school started in September. I leaped out of my seat. "That's where I belong this summer!" I exclaimed to Penny. "I'm working on a doctorate in higher education—what more important place could I be than in Washington, D.C., working as part of the President's Commission on Campus Unrest?" It wasn't as starry-eyed an ambition as it might seem, because I knew Charlie McWhorter.

I had met Charlie at Interlochen when I was sixteen. He was an Interlochen trustee and took a special interest in young men whom he considered to have leadership potential. I was privileged to have been one of those Charlie considered a future leader, and we had kept in touch since that summer. One of the best connectors of all time, Charlie had by then become one of the most important people in the Republican Party. David Broder, *Washington Post* journalist and "dean" of the Washington, D.C., press corps, would later claim that the party's most valuable asset in the post-Watergate era was Charlie's rolodex.

So, on that Friday night in June 1970 I called Charlie. "How," I asked, "does somebody with no Republican credentials, who has been a Vietnam War protester and canvasser for Eugene McCarthy, get a job in a Republican administration working on the President's Commission on Campus Unrest?" He responded, "Be in my office on Monday morning ready to tell me what you know about the subject."

The following Monday I spent an hour in his office at the AT&T building in New York telling him what I knew. Fortunately, I had helped several of my friends at Michigan through their doctoral dissertations on student beliefs and political involvement, and was able to convey this to Charlie. Charlie was convinced I knew enough that he could vouch for me. Before I left his office, Charlie called Gov. William Scranton of Pennsylvania, whom Nixon had just named to chair the commission. "Bill, I have a young man here," he began, "whom I'd like to recommend for the staff of the Commission you'll be leading." After I returned to Ann Arbor from New York, I received a call from the White House. I was told to be in Washington the next day, and to bring a suit and tie. I went down to Wagner's clothing store on South State Street, bought a tan summer suit, and headed off to Washington.

two
Washington, D.C.

Upon arriving in Washington in the early summer of 1970 I needed to learn quickly the basics of how government works. The Commission on Campus Unrest to which I was assigned as a staff member was supposed to finish its investigation in a matter of months, not years. Aware of this time constraint, people were helpful because they understood the importance of everyone on the commission staff getting up to speed. In just a few weeks, seasoned professionals Russell Edgerton and Martin Kramer in the Department of Health, Education, and Welfare and congressional staffers Bob Andringa and Harry Hogan helped stuff my head with as much knowledge as I might have gleaned during a semester-long course in government policies and practices.

Before long, I got bitten by the Potomac bug. Washington was where the action was, but it was also a beautiful city with parks, monuments, museums, fascinating people, and history everywhere. I found it irresistible. I had originally planned to return to Ann Arbor to begin work on my dissertation after my work on the commission was complete, but now I was having second thoughts. To complicate matters, Penny had received a grant from the Rockefeller Foundation and a teaching assistantship that would finance her doctor of musical arts degree at the University of Michigan. Penny and I talked it over. She generously offered to move with me to Washington. "Fisch, if that is where you should be," she said, "I can always enroll at Catholic University or the University of Maryland and work on my doctorate there." It was decided: we would move to Washington. The chair of my dissertation committee, James. L. Miller Jr., who was also the

director of the Center for the Study of Higher Education, not only supported the decision but put my name in for a position in D.C.

Professor Miller's recommendation netted me my first job in Washington: a four-year appointment as regional conference director of the American Association for Higher Education (AAHE), a new position funded by
a Kellogg Foundation grant. I started in September 1970, working out of
the National Center for Higher Education at One Dupont Circle. My mission was to find ways to engage the AAHE membership in conference set-
tings beyond the big annual conference held in Chicago each March. The
idea was to expand the membership and to provide greater value by giving members the opportunity to convene at lower cost in locations within
driving distance of their homes. With income assured for at least a few
years, Penny and I decided to really set down roots. Offered a loan from
my parents to cover the down payment, we bought a house on Columbia
Pike in Fairfax County in northern Virginia.

Washington, D.C., was not then known as an arts mecca, but, lucky for
us, our arrival in the nation's capital coincided with a period during which
a long-running effort to make the Washington, D.C., region as much a cul-
tural hub as a political one began to bear fruit. In early June 1971, the Wolf
Trap National Park for the Performing Arts in Vienna, Virginia, had its
inaugural performance featuring Van Cliburn, and Penny and I were there.
Soon thereafter, work on the John F. Kennedy Center for the Performing
Arts was completed. The grand opening concert—the world premiere of
Leonard Bernstein's *Mass*—was scheduled for September 8. Penny and
I wanted desperately to be present on that historic night, but we didn't
move quickly enough to get our tickets. Fortunately, after a long wait in
line, we were able to purchase what we were told were the last two available seats: very expensive obstructed-view box seats. The performance
was memorable for many reasons—the music, its message, the massive
number of people who performed. We noticed that Jackie Kennedy, who
commissioned the work, and Bernstein, who composed it, were both sitting in the President's Box on the same level as we were (President Nixon
did not attend the premiere out of courtesy to Jackie Kennedy, as he felt
"it really should be her night"). We were just thrilled to be there. It felt
right for us two arts lovers to be present at these openings of important
performing arts centers.

While I organized conferences for AAHE, Penny pursued a varied if
busy life working on her doctorate, playing in several performing ensem-

The Washington Post

TUESDAY, OCTOBER 30, 1973

New Fischer Composition Premiered at Georgetown

by Paul Humer
Washington Post Music Critic

WASHINGTON, Oct. 30— A new composition that can only be described as a masterpiece premiered today at the maternity ward of the Georgetown University Hospital. The performance, under the direction of Dr. Lowell Schwab, featured the composers themselves, Ken and Penny Fischer.

Most of the solo work was delivered by Penny with outstanding virtuosity while Ken supplied background support.

"That's what we had in mind when we conceived the piece nine months ago," said Ken. "Penny does that sort of thing so much better than I can."

"It took a lot of labor but it was worth every minute," Penny added.

The Fischers, glowingly happy over the success of their first composition, are products of the Lamaze Conservatory of Music, which stresses well rehearsed performances.

Their beautiful composition (weighing 8 lbs. and measuring 20 in.) miraculously sprang to life in the final movement with a resounding clapping theme followed by a glorious *tremolo fortissimo* vocal solo.

While future music scholars will refer to the composition as Fischer Opus 1, the public is expected to call the work by its more popular name, Matthew David.

Birth announcement of Matthew David Fischer (Opus 1) with a nod to Washington Post music critic Paul Hume.

bles, and giving private lessons. After about a year of study at Catholic University of America in the heart of D.C., she switched to the University of Maryland in College Park. In the summer of 1972, she went to Nice, France, for several weeks to study with Jean-Pierre Rampal, the famous French flutist.

Our lives changed dramatically when our son, Matt, was born on October 30, 1973, three years after we moved to Washington. As my mother had predicted, my experience helping to care for my baby sister, Martha, when I was 12 had prepared me well for the work of involved fatherhood.

When Matt arrived I was already an old pro at changing diapers and pre-paring bottles and all that stuff.

While it was common at that time for fathers to be so career focused that they spent precious little time with their children, I set a rather different course early in Matt's life. Penny was still playing gigs and going to rehearsals and it often fell to me to be Matt's caretaker. This didn't always mean we had to stay at home. On September 24, 1974, when Matt was 10 months old, Penny had our one car out on a gig and I was with Matt at our home in northern Virginia. Watching the sports news, I learned that Detroit Tigers right fielder Al Kaline—my boyhood hero growing up in the Detroit area—was playing that night in Baltimore, which happened to be his hometown. He was at 2,999 hits and would be retiring from the game in just a few more days. I had to be at that game because it was likely to be the night Kaline would become the 12th major leaguer to reach the milestone of 3,000 hits. I called a friend who grew up in Detroit and understood the significance of this evening. I offered to buy his ticket, cover the gas, do whatever it would take to get him to give me and Matt a ride to Baltimore. He agreed, but we got a late start. When Kaline came to bat for the first time, we were still on the Baltimore-Washington Parkway, listening to the game on the radio. I asked my friend to pull off to the side of the road. I got out of the car, got on my knees, and prayed for an out. Thank God, Kaline got out. Once we arrived at the stadium and found our seats above first base, it was the fourth inning and time for Kaline to bat the second time. I pointed Matt's head toward home plate as Kaline approached the batter's box. He doubled on the first pitch, and we went nuts along with the rest of the crowd. Thereafter, I loved being able to say that both Matt and I were there on September 24, 1974, when Al Kaline got his 3,000th hit.[1]

By the fall of 1974, I had organized nearly 100 successful conferences for AAHE. With this track record, I was approached by Samuel Halperin at the Institute for Educational Leadership at George Washington University and by Russell Edgerton at the Fund for the Improvement of Postsecond-ary Education. They were looking for someone to head a new program, the Postsecondary Education Convening Authority (PECA). They wanted someone who could put on conferences at which college leaders, public officials, and researchers would be engaged to discuss issues of public policy in higher education. They liked what I had done at AAHE and hired me as director of PECA toward the end of 1974.

Having gained a great deal of knowledge about conferences in my

AAHE job and having learned about group process at workshops sponsored by NTL Institute, I found myself challenging the conventional wisdom about meetings and how they were supposed to work. I moved in this direction at least partly because I was predisposed to what people today call "thinking outside the box," but it was also because I took seriously the idea that when people get together for a meeting they should feel engaged. Why have a keynote speaker if the knowledge is in the room? Why not tap into that knowledge and at the same time have fun with it? Why set the room up theater-style when people want to meet each other? As I experimented with different alternatives, I hit on something that met with good success: replacing the keynote address with a dramatic presentation featuring the conference attendees themselves. The basic idea was that the convening organization or institution would put on a play about its past, present, and future, with me as facilitator.

I used a standard approach each time. I would visit the client and ask three questions: "Where have you been, where are you now, and where are you headed?" Then I would begin to imagine a way to present the key ideas that emerged as a theatrical drama. I would outline five acts: one taking place ten years back, another five years back, another three days after the conference event that was taking place, a fourth one five years out, and a final act ten years out.

Then I would write the scenarios, figuring out what needed to happen in each of the five acts and the characters that needed to appear in each scene. I would spend the evening before the presentation assisting the actors, whom I had recruited by phone from the membership of the organization, in creating the dialogue. I did not write a script. I put down on paper only what characters would be in the scene and a description of what needed to happen in the five minutes or so between the beginning and end of the scene. The actors created the script.

Utilizing the conceit of *Our Town*, Thornton Wilder's classic play, I'd play the role of the narrator, summarizing the previous scene and setting up the next one. I recruited a person from the organization who could play light music on a piano while I spoke. The audience got to see people they knew playing different characters, which helped them open up to seeing themselves, their roles, and their organization in new ways.

Although this was an unconventional way to begin a conference, it got a lot of people involved immediately. It helped people already invested in an organization envision their own future, engaging them to frame it in a

Family portrait, mid-
1970s.

way that would be helpful to them. It was a fun, creative activity. Participation was the key.

In the summer of 1975, when Matt was 22 months old, Penny was
offered the opportunity to spend two weeks at the Harvey Sollberger Flute
Farm in Upstate New York. Harvey Sollberger was a contemporary flutist
and composer. There had been a robust interest in contemporary music
at the University of Michigan's School of Music, where she'd earned her
master's degree, and her interest in it had continued to grow while she was
doing her doctoral work. At the Flute Farm she would be living in a barn
with the other workshop participants. It would be an intensive dive into
contemporary/experimental flute music and performance—something
she really wanted to do. The same two weeks I was supposed to be doing
some work for PECA that would take me to Interlochen, Michigan; Sara-
toga Springs, New York; and Tanglewood in Lenox, Massachusetts. Penny
and I concluded that it would make sense for Matt to come with me so
that Penny could focus entirely on her flute playing.

The trip went fine with Matt in tow, and the experience initiated an arrangement that would hold for several years: when I went on a business trip, Matt would frequently come along. I was very comfortable with Matt, but I also had a job to do and partners to whom I was responsible. I would not take him on a trip with me unless I knew the client did not have a problem with it and that Matt could be well taken care of when I was working. It was the beginning of a great life adventure.

An example of how my travel with Matt played out involved a visit to Berkeley, California, to work with the Educational Testing Service. I called my contact at Educational Testing Service, reassured him that he was my top priority, and asked if he knew of someone who might advise me on finding child care for my three-year-old son for the three days I was consulting. He connected me with a colleague whose child was in a preschool in Berkeley, and arrangements were made for Matt to join the preschool. Matt was an adaptable kid, used to being in a variety of different environments, so within 30 minutes or less, as I observed him at the school, he was in the groove with the other kids. He enjoyed three days at the preschool and three evenings with his dad visiting the sights on each side of the Bay.

During a period of about four years, Matt and I built a special relationship during our travels to New York, Texas, Colorado, Florida, and other states. These adventures also allowed Penny more time to work on her doctorate at Maryland, perform in ensembles around the D.C. area, and teach her private flute students.

It was during this time, in 1975, that I learned a lesson about the status of the arts in American life. I was convening an important PECA meeting in San Francisco that included Clark Kerr, former University of California president, and other high-profile education and government leaders. I had engaged a string quartet from the San Francisco Conservatory to play during the conference. The quartet had agreed to play for the nominal fee of $100, which was all I could offer given the lack of any funds in the budget for entertainment. The quartet's performance was well received and many participants commented on how it enhanced the conference. I covered the payment to the musicians myself. Later, George Washington University denied me reimbursement for the expense, believing it to be frivolous. It wasn't a great deal of money, but I decided to take a stand on it as a matter of principle. I sent a letter to the university asking that they reconsider. "If my own university does not see the value of including the arts at a conference on higher education," I wrote to the finance officials, "then who can we count on to encourage and support creative expression in our culture and in the education of our children?" I eventually won the argument and I was reimbursed the $100, but the ordeal put me face to face with the dominant attitude that the arts exist on the fringe and are less valuable than other activities. I realized then that engaging artists in our lives was something I would often need to fight for.

During this time, I was able to keep up my French horn chops playing with my friends in "Goliard East." We would rehearse for a few hours each weekend and perform at an occasional alumni, church, or conference gig. I also put together an informal woodwind quintet made up of fellow musicians in the neighborhood who would play during lunch in my office at 17th and K Streets. We called ourselves the Brown Bagatelles. At about the same time I organized a madrigal singing group, after I received a collection of madrigals from an acquaintance in the Williamsburg Madrigal Singers. We sang regularly on Sunday afternoons and called ourselves, appropriately enough, the Sunday Afternoon Madrigal Singers. We also performed on occasion but, like performing with the Goliards, it was mainly for our own amateur enjoyment. On the occasion of the Bicentennial, in 1976, I organized a 24-hour party for the madrigal group during which we turned back the clock 200 years in every way we could. We rented Belmont, an early 18th-century country manor between Baltimore and Washington, wore period clothing, enjoyed a feast similar to what would have been served in 1776, sang madrigals in candlelight, and danced some of the contra dances of the period well past midnight.

The year 1976 was when I met Patrick Hayes, a legendary impresario who ran the Washington Performing Arts Society. As a young man, Patrick had been shaped by one of the most important events in the history of performing arts presenting. In 1939, Marian Anderson, the great contralto, was denied the opportunity to sing in Constitution Hall because the Daughters of the American Revolution, which ran the venue, had a clause in its contract specifying that blacks were not permitted to perform there. This discrimination so incensed the Roosevelts that Eleanor Roosevelt resigned from the Daughters of the American Revolution and the president and Mrs. Roosevelt offered to present Ms. Anderson on the steps of the Lincoln Memorial. Over 75,000 people heard her perform. This event had quite an impact on Patrick. He became determined to do all he could to erase the racial divide in the arts.

In 1953, after he and his colleagues were finally successful in getting the

Daughters of the American Revolution to change its discriminatory policies, Patrick became the first person to present Marian Anderson in recital at Constitution Hall. To signify that the arts were for everybody, Patrick developed an inclusion policy called EINO—Everybody In, Nobody Out.

In 1976 Patrick began advising a small group that was trying to save the Western Presbyterian Church at the corner of 19th and H Streets. The church was losing membership and the International Monetary Fund, whose large office building was next door, was eager to buy the property to expand its operation. A British gentleman named A. Graham Down, who was moonlighting as the church's choir director and organist, suggested that a good means of inspiring people to save the church, and of publicizing its cause, would be to have free chamber music at the church at noontime. That's what got me and three other music lovers involved in helping Graham realize his vision. Seeing myself as an enabler, I arranged for the five of us to meet with Patrick. He interrogated our plans, suggested that our group form under the umbrella of the Washington Performing Arts Society, and set up appointments with the Cafritz and Kiplinger Foundations.

Soon we had $25,000 to help us get started what we called Music at Noon. The noontime concerts were a success, and the beginning of a renaissance for the church. Soon after the concerts began, the church established Miriam's Kitchen, which at its height fed 250 homeless people each weekday morning. Alcoholics Anonymous eventually offered multiple meetings there each week. The church became a dynamic community resource in Washington with a strong link to nearby George Washington University, where both Penny and I had affiliations.

Everyone in the organizing group served as volunteers for the first few years. Later, when we had 10 times as many musical groups applying to be presented as we could accommodate, we felt badly about no one in the organization having time to write back to them; musicians deserved to be treated better than that. At this point we determined that a paid managing director was needed to handle such things, a responsibility I was asked to take on.[2]

Though I was actively involved with the Western Presbyterian Church through Music at Noon, Penny and I were congregants at another socially engaged church, the John Calvin Presbyterian Church of Annandale, Virginia. After a life of continuous involvement in religion—and a period during which I seriously considered attending seminary—I had by this time evolved an awareness that faith should be something that unites people rather than driving them apart into groups where each asserts the superiority of its beliefs. Looking at the rest of the world and its diversity of faiths, I began to ask myself, "What is it we all have in common, as opposed to what makes us different?" The idea that resonated for me, and seemed common to every faith, was the Golden Rule: Do unto others as you would have them do unto you. I carried this awareness forward with me as my work led me toward increasing contact with artists and audiences from a wide variety of cultural and faith backgrounds.

By 1978, after four years as director of PECA, I had developed a reputation as a guy who could design and carry out conferences that dealt with important subjects but were highly engaging for attendees because they prioritized people and involved participation, music, simulations, games, and sometimes sports. The federal grant that funded the PECA program was coming to an end, however, and I had no idea what I would do next. In July of that year, I visited with Anne Wilson Schaef, a friend, best-selling author, Fund for the Improvement of Secondary Education grantee, and consultant who lived in Boulder, Colorado. She organized a dinner at Fez, a Moroccan restaurant in Denver, where she introduced me to Dr. Robert Leichtman, an author and medical intuitive. As we awaited our dinner, Dr. Leichtman took me to a corner and invited me to put my hands in his for a few seconds. I did so, and when he released my hands he looked me in the eye and said, "It's time to get off soft money, and it will all work out in December." I wasn't quite sure what to make of that, but I took it in and waited to see what would happen.

Something else significant happened a few months later. In the space of a single week, the heads of four national associations who had attended and enjoyed PECA events that I had organized made separate calls to me inviting me to serve as a meeting consultant for their respective organizations. The message was clear: I had a ready-made basis for a consulting business. So that's what I decided to do. In December, just as the grant supporting PECA ran out, I secured my first client, the Learner's Co-op. They put me on a $3,000-per-month retainer for a year, a guaranteed income stream that was enough to get me started. I did the same kind of work I had been doing, designing and managing conferences and special events, but now I was working for myself. My work for the Learners' Co-op allowed me time to secure and work for other clients, including the four national higher education associations, and eventually individual colleges and universities, other nonprofit associations, and several corporations.

I'd had enough experience in the business by then to write a book, *Little Big Winners: 77 Ideas for a Better Conference.* It was published in 1979. Idea 27 suggested that everyone participating in a conference send in a photograph and bits of personal information they would want to share and that this material be gathered together into a "face book." With the face book available, you could minimize the time people spent jockeying around and finding out where they fit in. Much later, when reminded about Idea 27, I realized I should have trademarked "face book."

As I built my business, Matt entered school and Penny continued working part-time on her doctorate, researching and writing a dissertation on the French flutist, conductor, and composer Philippe Gaubert. She tried to limit her visits to College Park to one per week because of the length and stress of the commute. In addition to being a mom and graduate student, she had as many as 40 private students at a time and frequent performances and rehearsals. At one point, she participated in seven different professional ensembles. In 1980, in addition to everything else, she began teaching at George Washington University.

Late in 1981, we learned that Jean-Pierre Rampal was scheduled to perform with and conduct the National Symphony Orchestra at the Kennedy Center in early January. Penny and Jean-Pierre had maintained a strong friendship since Penny's session as his student in 1972, and the three of us had spent time together more than once when he was Washington. Knowing that the scheduled date of the concert—January 7—was Jean-Pierre's 60th birthday, Penny concocted a plan.

On the day of the concert, we arranged to pick up Jean-Pierre at the Watergate Hotel and ferry him the very short distance to the Kennedy Center. When we entered the backstage area, Penny gave Jean-Pierre a fabricated reason for needing to go to the lobby. As he opened the door, 60 flutists launched into a rousing rendition of "Happy Birthday." He loved it. We were not aware that among the many concertgoers waiting in the lobby at the time was someone quite struck by the idea of a large ensemble of flutists marking an important day for a celebrity.

Not long after the concert and Rampal birthday tribute at the Kennedy Center at the beginning of 1982, my brother Jerry, along with a minister and a public-relations guy, presented the a cappella sextet the King's Singers at Orchestra Hall in Detroit under the auspices of Brethren Productions. Jerry and his wife, Cathie, had discovered the group during a two-year work assignment in England and had fallen in love with them. When Penny and I heard them, we fell in love with them too. The six members, all choral scholars at King's College at Cambridge University, were delightful human beings who could sing any style of music in any language, didn't need amplification because of their well-trained voices and impeccable diction, and knew just how to use their understated British wit between pieces. The concert that Jerry copresented was a great success despite the fact that Detroit, in economic decline for some years, had been particularly hard hit by the recession that had begun in early 1980. Watching from Washington, D.C., I thought, "if Jerry can be successful presenting the King's Singers in a recession-ridden Detroit, imagine what we could do in recession-proof Washington."

The King's Singers had never performed in a large venue in Washington, D.C. When I talked to two of the principal presenters in our area about bringing them to the Kennedy Center, neither expressed interest. So I decided to do it myself. Friends considered me a pretty good organizer, and I was making a living as an independent consultant helping organizations design their meetings and special events. I figured I could find some extra time to mount a Kennedy Center event, so in late February 1982, I got in touch with Beverly Taylor, the King's Singers' U.S. "agent-enthusiast." Bev told me that the guys would indeed like to perform at the Kennedy Center and would be available during February the next year.

I went to the Kennedy Center to see about booking the Concert Hall. I had never presented a concert like this before. When I sat down with the person who keeps the calendar, she greeted me with a look that seemed to say, "Now who the heck are you?" She told me that my priority for access to dates in the hall was about as low as you can get given all the established groups that would have a higher priority. "Well, what dates *can* I get?," I asked. "For you, my friend, Mondays in February," she replied. "There's the 7th, the 14th, the 21st, the . . ." I jumped up and said, "You mean the 14th of February is available! No one's taken Valentine's Day yet? Put me down!"

Then she told me the Kennedy Center would need $10,000 up front to secure the date. I took a deep breath. No way could I put up that kind of money. It was coming out of my own pocket, and I just didn't have it. I sat back, looked at her, and said, "Tell me a little bit about you." She looked at me as though to say, "Now what does that have to do with anything?" I admitted that I was new to all of this, and she seemed to soften. She explained that she was new to her job, too, having recently come to Washington from Hanover, New Hampshire, where her ex-husband was on the Dartmouth faculty. I sat up and asked, "You wouldn't happen to know my brother Norman Fischer, would you?" She smiled. "I know Norman Fischer and all of the Concord String Quartet in residence at Dartmouth. I love your brother." She changed her story. "Look, instead of $10,000, why don't you give me $2,500. That guarantees the hall rental, and that should be enough." I called Bev Taylor later that day, and we struck a deal. The King's Singers would perform in the 2,759-seat Kennedy Center Concert Hall on Valentine's Day in 1983—Monday, February 14.

I had a lot of work to do. I realized that, first and foremost, I needed to find a private box office so that I could collect ticket revenues to pay for the promotional brochure and other expenses that I would incur in advance of the event. If I used the Kennedy Center's box office exclusively, I wouldn't be able to access those funds until after the concert.

I put out the word to 11 nonprofit organizations that I thought might want to raise some money. I offered the same arrangement to all of them. Their responsibility would be to help sell tickets. I'd pay all the direct expenses of putting on the event—the artists' fee, the promotional brochure, postage costs, hall rental, stagehands, and so forth. Since that meant I was taking on the full financial risk, I'd next pay myself $10,000. The organization would get all the profits above that—which, if the concert sold out, could be as much as $20,000. I made it clear that 1,700 to 1,800 seats had to be sold before the organization would see any money at all. But it would receive the full amount of each ticket sold between 1,800 and a sold-out house of 2,759. This arrangement gave the organization a clear incentive to work hard until the very last seat was sold.

One group, the Alexandria Harmonizers, leaped at the chance to participate. It was a 170-member men's barbershop chorus based in Alexandria, Virginia. Their leader Chuck Harner told me that they had two reasons for wanting to get involved. First was to make some money to help cover their expenses to the barbershoppers' convention the following summer in Seattle, where they would compete for the world championship. Second was to gain some visibility and respect by associating themselves with one of the world's finest men's vocal ensembles.[3]

The Harmonizers regularly sold out each of their own concerts using an excellent mailing list and an unusual but highly effective box office approach. The "box office" was the home of one of their retired members, Linton Reed. He'd sit at home all day, receiving mail orders and taking credit-card orders over the phone. He was pleasant with the patrons, meticulous with the figures, and trustworthy with the money. We agreed that we'd run Linton's box office for about four months prior to the concert, and Linton offered his services free of charge as a contribution to the Harmonizers. Everything was set.

That autumn, we began working on promoting the show. The initial approach we took was to mail a brochure to everyone on the Harmonizers' mailing list and to other barbershoppers, choral groups, and church choirs in the region. In addition, I worked with every school district music supervisor and got their help putting the brochure, along with a group-sales form, into the hands of every music teacher.

One day that November, after the first phase of the publicity campaign for the King's Singers' concert had been under way for a while, Penny, Matt, and I were running late for a flight to Paris. Wrapping up her doctoral dissertation, Penny had felt the need to verify some facts at the Bibliothèque nationale de France, and it seemed a great excuse for all three of us to go to Paris for Thanksgiving and celebrate the imminent completion of Penny's doctorate. We jammed into our 1965 VW bug, surrounded by luggage, and just as I was about to speed to Dulles Airport, 23 miles away, I realized I had forgotten to pack something. I ran back into the house and the phone rang. My first thought was to ignore it, but I picked up the receiver. "Hello," said a cheery but formal-sounding woman, "this is Muffie Brandon, Nancy Reagan's social secretary. Is Penny Fischer there?" After taking a second to process the situation, I told Ms. Brandon I would get Penny on the line. I yelled out to the car, "Penny, it's the White House!" She yelled back, "Tell them I'll call them when we get back." "No!," I shouted. "It's the WHITE HOUSE!" She tromped into the house certain we would now miss our flight. Ms. Brandon proceeded to explain to Penny that she had been in the lobby of the Kennedy Center when the flutists played the surprise tribute to Jean-Pierre Rampal's 60th birthday. "I was waiting to go into the concert and I heard these flutes," said Ms. Brandon. "They were just magnificent. It would be wonderful if you would organize a flute choir for President Reagan's holiday party for the cabinet and senior staff." Penny knew just how to respond. "We're late for a flight. Let's leave it this way. Yes, I can help you with this. How about we talk about the details when I get back?" Ms. Brandon said OK, and we dashed back to the car and took off. We made the flight and had a great time in Paris.

After we got back home Penny organized a group of 16 flutists to play for the president's holiday party. We agreed that she needed a manager for this event, so I volunteered, happy that I'd be able to return to the White House for another visit 20 years after the 1962 Interlochen experience.

As the date of the King's Singers' concert approached, we knew that what we really needed to do was get the group's music on the radio. Only a few people in Washington knew who these guys were, but, we figured, as soon as they hear them, they'll love them.

One radio guy who did know their work was Robert Aubry Davis of Washington's public radio station, WETA-FM. Robert was delighted to give the King's Singers some airtime. He not only played their music frequently but also mentioned the concert date and Linton Reed's phone number. I gave WETA-FM's morning drive-time host Bill Cerri a recording of one of the King's Singers' favorites, "You Are the New Day," and he began to play it every morning. The first time he did so, 33 people called the station. "Who are these guys?," they asked. "Where can I get that record?" "Can you play that song again?" After the station let me know about this interest, I duplicated several hundred copies of the words to "New Day," put them on stationery that gave the date, time, and place of the concert (plus Linton Reed's phone number) and gave them to the station to send to the hundreds of people who requested them.[4]

The Harmonizers had a relationship with another station, WMAL, the area's top-rated AM station. They knew the afternoon drive-time team, especially John Lyon, who happily promoted all the Harmonizers' own concerts. We got John copies of the King's Singers' more popular albums, and he began to play these recordings almost daily, also mentioning details of the concert. Soon he and his listeners discovered the King's Singers' versions of ABBA's "Money, Money, Money" and Kenny Rogers's "The Gambler", and the results were the same as they been when WETA played "New Day." I got King's Singers' albums to several other stations. Ticket sales began to take off.

I began to get a little anxious about my financial exposure. What if we had to cancel the show for some reason and refund all the tickets? I'd be on the hook for a substantial sum. So I decided to take out an insurance policy that protected me against the loss of gross ticket sales should the event have to be cancelled by a reason beyond my control. The risk I imagined was the possibility of the King's Singers getting stranded in Minneapolis—it would be winter there, after all—and not being able to arrive in Washington on time.

On February 2, 12 days before the concert, we'd sold about 1,400 tickets, about half the house. Lots of group sales had come in from choral groups. We hadn't bought any advertising yet. I had arranged with Bev Taylor and the King's Singers to come to Washington that day for a pre-tour press conference at the National Press Club and a record signing, along with a television appearance on Maury Povich's local morning talk show, *Panorama*, the next day. February 2 happened also to be day of the huge parade celebrating the Washington Redskins' 27–17 Super Bowl victory over the Miami Dolphins three days before on January 30. Everybody loved the hometown team, and everybody was celebrating.

I picked the guys up at National Airport and quickly got them to the borrowed van I used for transportation. There they were, finally: Jeremy Jackman, Al Hume, Bill Ives, Tony Holt, Simon Carrington, and Colin Mason. After loading up their luggage, I asked them to listen carefully to what I was about to say. I handed each of them the sheet music for "Hail to the Redskins," the football team's fight song, known and loved by everybody in Washington. I then played them a taped version of the song by the Singing Sergeants of the U.S. Air Force. I urged them to learn the song and incorporate it into their Press Club program. If they did so, I said, they'd be a big hit, especially on this day, and we'd sell hundreds of tickets.

At the National Press Club event, the guys are scheduled to sing a couple of pieces, be interviewed by the press, then end with two songs. Reporters from the *Washington Post* and several other papers are present, along with a couple of folks from the National Endowment for the Arts, Robert Aubry Davis, and a few other radio types. There's an audience stocked with friends and family members. The guys sing beautifully and handle the interview superbly.

Now it's time to wrap it up with two songs. They announce the first one: Rossini's *The Barber of Seville Overture.* It's a big hit with the crowd. Moving to the edge of my seat, I get a big grin on my face as I wait for the introduction to the final song. "For our final piece today, we'd like to do a popular 16th-century madrigal, Thomas Morley's 'Now Is the Month of Maying.'" I stare at them from the front row, in shock. Don't these guys know anything about marketing? Why didn't they listen to me? As I sit back and shake my head in disbelief, they begin, indeed, to sing "Now Is the Month of Maying." Two verses and two choruses. Then, without missing a beat, they segue into "Hail to the Redskins" instead of the third verse of the madrigal. After a moment of confusion, the audience goes absolutely wild, and I with them. I realize that the guys had spent the four hours between the van ride and the press appearance arranging "Hail to the Redskins" as an adaptation of the madrigal. The next day on Maury Povich's *Panorama* show they do the same thing, and Linton Reed's phone is ablaze with calls.

On Thursday, February 10, four days before the concert, we had reached the important 1,800-ticket threshold. The Harmonizers would now start to make some money with the sale of every additional ticket. Whew! But it is beginning to snow. By midnight there are 20 inches of snow on the ground, the largest accumulation in decades. Washington doesn't know how to handle snow except to close everything—the schools, the government, the Kennedy Center. Not just on Friday, but on Saturday, and Sunday, too. We don't sell a single ticket through the Kennedy Center box office during the weekend because of the closure. (But Linton Reed keeps his box office open and continues to sell tickets.) The one newspaper ad we had decided to run, in the Entertainment Section of the *Washington Post* on Friday, February 11, isn't seen by many people because only half of the Friday papers get to their destination, and the phone number in the ad is for the shuttered Kennedy Center box office.

On the morning of Monday, February 14, the day I'd been anticipating for a year, the weather report tells me that a storm brewing in the Carolinas will hit Washington in the afternoon and bring more snow. The city is still digging itself out from Thursday's storm. The schools are still closed and the federal government is on "liberal leave," meaning that if it's going to be a huge hassle to get to work, you don't have to show up. At least the Kennedy Center has reopened.

The guys arrive at the airport from Minneapolis and I pick them up in the same borrowed van and take them to the Watergate Hotel, where I'd been able to get each of them a nice suite at a regular room price. The guys are relaxed and happy. I am relieved that they are in Washington, the Kennedy Center is open, and the storm is blowing out to sea over southern Virginia. At 3:15 p.m. the guys and I walk to the Kennedy Center Concert Hall to begin the standard one-hour sound and light check. I introduce the fellows to Paul Simerman, manager of the Concert Hall, and to the two stagehands working the show.

At 3:45, while the guys are in the middle of rehearsing a tune, the lights go out. All the lights. The stagehands check backstage and discover that the power is out in the hall. I look outside the window and see no lights at the Watergate. We learn that a transformer has blown nearby and that much of Foggy Bottom is out of power. The exit lights provide enough illumination for the guys to continue the rehearsal. I find Paul Simerman and ask him how long he expects the power to be out. "This has happened only once before, Ken," he says, "and it was 24 hours before power was restored." He tells me he'll do everything he can, but that if there's no power, there's no show. The guys finish their rehearsal, walk back to the Watergate, climb the stairs to the suites, and prepare their toast using the heat from the candles. I remain at the Kennedy Center to stay on top of the situation.

Three other events are scheduled for the Kennedy Center that evening—one at 7:30, two at 8:00. Paul and I agree to meet with the other presenters and hall managers at 6:15 p.m. to determine the fate of the evening's events. Members of the press start to gather near the Kennedy Center. Satellite vans and remote news teams are preparing for live broadcasts to report on the power failure. I call the King's Singers and ask if they would prepare a ditty about the power failure that they can sing in front of the cameras. I figure if we were going to have to cancel the concert we might as well turn the crisis into an opportunity and give the guys free exposure on TV. Someone asks me how I'm managing to stay calm. I smile, tell them something vague, and don't mention the insurance policy that's protecting my financial investment.

At 6:15, we learn that the utility people are working on the problem, but there is still no power. We begin our meeting with the other presenters. They all decide to cancel their shows. All eyes are now on me. My show is scheduled to begin at 8:30. What am I going to do? Paul and I huddle for a minute. We decide to give it another half hour, and I announce that we'll have a decision at 6:45. That way, if I have to announce a cancellation, I'll still have 15 minutes to get the guys on each of the local affiliates, now positioned adjacent to each other in front of the Kennedy Center, before the national news comes on at 7:00 p.m.

By 6:30, word is out among the employees of the Kennedy Center that there's this one guy—me—holding everybody up from being able to go home early. Scores of people come out of the woodwork from the kitchens, backstage, parking garages, and gift shops. They all want me to say "Let's go home." But I'm thinking of all the groups of barbershoppers to whom we've sold group tickets, coming from as far away as Pennsylvania. They're already on the road. I'm thinking of all the school choirs and church choirs in the area whose buses are just now picking them up. And I'm thinking of all the single ticket buyers who'll be leaving their homes in the next half hour. I may still appear calm, but inside the anxiety is mounting.

At 6:41 p.m. exactly, just as Chuck and I are strategizing how to staff each entrance to explain to our patrons that we've had to cancel the concert because of a power blackout, the lights come on. Tom Kendrick, second in command at the Center under Roger Stevens, calls the utility company and learns that they can't assure us that the transformer won't blow again. Tom, Paul, and I determine that we'll go ahead with the show and take our chances.

Tom and Paul make a quick determination that only a skeleton crew of Kennedy Center employees will be needed to staff our show. They dismiss the bartenders, the parking attendants, and most of the custodial staff, leaving a handful of people, plus the ushers. Most everyone now has a smile on his or her face. A team of our volunteers goes to the phones and, with help from the Kennedy Center media relations people, they call all the media saying that even though the other shows at the Kennedy Center are cancelled, the King's Singers are still on. Another team goes outside and tells the same thing to the TV news crews, who report it to their listeners. And another group is dispatched to each of the entrances of the Kennedy Center to encourage those patrons coming to attend one of the cancelled shows to buy tickets to our show with their refunds.

When the lights in the Concert House are dimmed to begin our concert at 8:30, there are 2,200 people in the hall. Probably 200 of them had arrived at the Center with no intention of attending our concert, yet there they are. The 2,000 others made their way through snow-covered streets or covered great distances to be here. I love every one of them. My wife and son, who provided so much encouragement over the past year, are at my side, and now the concert I'd been working so hard for is about to begin.

The guys put on a sensational performance. They do Paul Patterson's "Time Piece" and Thomas Tallis's *Lamentations of Jeremiah*. They sing 16th- and 17th-century madrigals and some of the Victorians like my favorite "Phyllis Is My Only Joy." They sing "Lazy Bones," "Just One of Those Things," and other popular tunes. They wrap it up with *The Barber of Seville* and a couple of encores.

At the after-show party in the Presidential Suite at the Watergate, everyone says how thrilled they are with the concert. The Alexandria Harmonizers and I made some money and we'd had a ball working together.

The King's Singers who performed at the Kennedy Center Concert Hall on Valentine's Day 1983. L, top to bottom: Anthony Holt, Jeremy Jackman, Alastair Hume. R, top to bottom, Simon Carrington, Bill Ives, Colin Mason.

We ask the Kings if we can present them again. Conversations begin about a possible October date later that year.

The next day, Matt stayed home from school and I slept in until about 9:00 a.m., which was probably a record for me. I scanned the papers and was gratified to see the critics using the words *perfect* and *perfection* to describe the show. "Avoiding constant superlatives is difficult if not impossible in describing the King's Singers' concert," wrote the critic in the *Washington Post.* "They really must be heard to be believed. But it hardly would do them justice merely to say that each selection technically was perfect. Their perfection also extended to areas such as phrasing, style, dynamic range, diction, and intonation—areas for which talent and hard work are required in equal measure." The *Washington Times* reviewer wrote that the "intrepidity" of those who braved the conditions to attend "was rewarded by a performance that was as close to perfection as anyone could ask." The critic writing for the *Columbia Flier* said that if you wanted to imagine the hypothetically "perfect" concert it "would be like the concert recently given at the Kennedy Center by the King's Singers." And for good measure he added that it "may well have been the best concert I've ever heard."

Doing the event taught me quite a few things about presenting a concert. I started to think that organizing and presenting musical performances might be an exciting way to make a living, rather than just a sideline. But for the time being, I was content with presenting concerts from time to time when the opportunities arose.

During the mid-1980s, I was very busy presenting performances at the Kennedy Center, pursuing my conference-design consulting business, and doing a great deal of volunteer work. In particular, I continued to work with Music at Noon and to serve on the boards of two musical organizations in Washington—the Levine School of Music and the Washington Bach Consort—which meant raising money for them and promoting their programs.[5] My involvement with the Bach Consort was a multifaceted family affair: my sister, Martha, and her husband, Bill Lutes, sang in the group's chorus, Penny played flute in the orchestra, and I was vice chair of the board.

With the Consort slated to perform in Leipzig on March 24, 1985 as part of a festival commemorating the 300th anniversary of Johann Sebastian Bach's birth, I worked with board chair Rosemary Monagan and others to raise funds to support the ensemble's travel. I also volunteered to host 80 additional people to accompany the 80 instrumentalists, singers, conductor, and staff on the trip, each of whom made a gift of $400 over the cost of the trip to help cover the costs for the ensemble. Among those 80 people were my parents and our son, Matt, who combined with Penny, Martha, Martha's husband Bill, and me to yield a seven-member Fischer family contingent. My father, a huge Bach fan and an amateur organist, was determined to be on the trip even though he was fighting cancer.

We were held up at the East German border on the morning of March 21, Bach's birthday. We missed the 10 a.m. birthday celebration in Bach's birthplace of Eisenach, arriving just as the ceremony was breaking up. Everyone else was leaving as our four buses drove up. We all gathered around the statue of Bach while I passed out sheet music I'd duplicated the night before in Kasel—of the chorale "Break Forth Oh Beauteous Heavenly Light." As we began to sing, the sun broke through the clouds and radiant light shone down on the statue. I'm not making this up. We were able to get through only one verse, given the deep emotion we all felt at that moment. Three days later, on March 24, the Washington Bach Consort was the featured ensemble at a performance in the Gewandhaus in Leipzig, the city in which Bach spent the latter part of his life. Dad told me afterward that being on this Bach pilgrimage with his family was one of the highlights of his life. (He would die two years later.)

In 1986 our 12-year-old son Matt, together with my wife Penny, called for a family council. In a kind and gentle way, but with a measure of firmness, they said it was time that we had more financial stability and security in our household. In short, it was time for Pops to consider getting a "real job" with a regular paycheck and benefits. There was acknowledgment that my consulting business had its ups and downs, and now that I was getting more involved in the arts, there was even greater risk. And there would be college tuition in six years. What they said, in such a touching way, made a lot of sense to me. From that moment forward, I was open to considering regular employment. I made it clear that it would have to be interesting and fun and that a measure of risk would be OK.

Shortly after our family council I got a phone call from Emmy Lewis, a friend from the board of the Washington Bach Consort. She was a skilled and highly successful direct-mail political fundraiser. She loved our son Matt and was a good family friend. She was calling me from Ann Arbor, where she was visiting her friend Lois Stegeman, a member of the board of directors of the University Musical Society of the University of Michigan. Lois had told her that UMS was looking for a new executive director—in fact, Lois herself was on the search committee. "Ken," Emmy told me, "your next job is in Ann Arbor—executive director of the University Musical Society." She emphasized that the search committee was working on the task as we spoke and that I should send them a resume as soon as possible. I did as she instructed and was soon contacted by a representative of the University Musical Society who told me I was being considered for the position.

I was excited about the prospect, for sure, but concerned that I really had no credentials to be a performing arts presenter at a highly regarded university presenting organization. I'd done some gigs at the Kennedy Center (about a dozen at that point), but I'd never run an organization with more than one employee and had never curated a performing arts season.

So I called Patrick Hayes and we set up a meeting. In my naivete, I asked him how I could get artists to come to Ann Arbor if I didn't have a personal connection with them. He explained that artists *want* to come perform at your venue, that you don't have to beg them to come, and that you communicate with them through artist managers. I responded that I didn't know any of these artist managers. "The artists want to come," he reminded me. "Their managers will be contacting you—you'd be at the University Musical Society, after all!" Over the course of our four-hour session I asked him all kinds of questions about the field and learned how the business of presenting ran from the guy who knew it all.

At the end of those four hours I asked humbly, "Patrick, do I have what it takes for the Ann Arbor job or not?" I'd warned him at the beginning of our meeting that I'd ask a question at the end requiring a completely honest answer. He responded enthusiastically, "You've got it, now go for it!"

With that endorsement from someone I trusted and respected, I went from having doubts to being absolutely confident I could do it. He gave me so much confidence, in fact, that if the search committee had called me on the phone at that moment I would have told them that they could stop the search because I'm their guy. After all, Patrick Hayes said I can do it, and he knows what he's talking about.

I didn't know where they were at in the search process. A few weeks later, in the early summer of 1986, still feeling confident, I called John Reed, the head of the search committee. "I'm driving to Interlochen and will be passing by Ann Arbor," I told him. "I'd be delighted to meet with the committee. It won't cost you a dime." He convened the committee. I thought the meeting went well. It was clear that they were taking my candidacy seriously and were interested in me.

A critical visit occurred over the weekend of October 11. Penny and I were ready to move if I were offered the job. We knew Ann Arbor and UMS well. Matt, on the other hand, was ambivalent. Just shy of 13, he saw that a full-time job for his dad would be a good thing for the family, but he wasn't entirely happy about leaving the Washington area and his friends. And his favorite teams were the Redskins and the Orioles. He had only ever lived in the Washington, D.C., area.

Penny and I checked the U-M football schedule and saw that the Michigan–Michigan State game would be at the Big House on October 11. We figured that once Matt had the experience of attending a game in the largest college stadium in the country, between two Big Ten rivals, he might begin to think differently about coming to Ann Arbor if and when the time came.

We didn't have tickets for the game. Penny, predicting that two tickets would be easier to obtain than three, offered to stay at the hotel. Matt and I headed for Michigan Stadium. We "worked the fences" looking for tickets, but the prices being asked were beyond our reach. When we found ourselves back at the entrance of the stadium empty-handed, I told Matt we should probably head back to the hotel.

Just then, two guys walked up to us, asking, "Are you a father and a son trying to get into the game?" I affirmed that status. "Are you willing to pay face value?," he asked. "You mean $18? Absolutely," I said. I showed him the money and he said, "Follow me." We headed off to Section 23 and found ourselves in Row 20, close to the field just to the right of the 50-yard line. Matt and I smiled, high-fived each other, hardly able to believe our good fortune. "How is it that you have such great seats?" I asked the man who sold us the tickets. "Oh, a relative of ours used to work in the athletics department," he said casually, "and we've kept these seats in the family." (I would find out 20 years later that the man who sold me the tickets was Jim Baird of Chicago, the grandnephew of Charles Baird, the first athletics director at U-M.)

We enjoyed the game immensely. Michigan beat Michigan State soundly 27–6, putting an exclamation point at the close of a memorable day. With Matt won over to the prospect of moving to Ann Arbor, all that was left was actually being offered the job. In late November, I was called in for one final meeting with the board.

Before I left our home in the D.C. area for that meeting in the UMS President's Office at Burton Memorial Tower, I called my good friend Jon McBride, a D.C.-based executive search consultant, to see if he had any last-minute advice. He told me I should not leave the interview until I had the answers to four questions: "What will be your title, to whom will you report, what will be the compensation, and, most importantly, how will they judge whether you're succeeding or failing?"

During the meeting, members of the board answered each of the first three questions. As we were wrapping up, they asked, "Is there anything else we should discuss?" That's when I asked, "How will you judge whether I'm succeeding or failing?" There was silence as they looked at one another uncomfortably, not sure who would respond. It didn't surprise me that they couldn't answer the question. Feeling their discomfort, I said, "It's OK that you might not have the answer right now. In fact, wouldn't it be better if we were to decide together how I will be evaluated? If I get the job, perhaps we could have a retreat in the fall and set some goals for the organization." They were clearly relieved to get off the hook. A few days later, when I was up at Interlochen for a meeting, I received a call from search committee chair John Reed inviting me to become the sixth leader of the University Musical Society. I thanked John and accepted with enthusiasm. I would begin June 1, 1987.

Notes

1. Thirty-three years later, in 2007, Matt and I got a photo with Al Kaline in Cooperstown, when Matt's boyhood hero, Cal Ripken Jr., was inducted into the Baseball Hall of Fame.

2. Thirteen years later, the International Monetary Fund came back and offered many millions for the property, much more than the $1 million offer in 1976. After much negotiation, the church eventually agreed, and over time a new Western Presbyterian Church was built at the corner of Virginia Avenue and 24th Street near the Watergate and the Kennedy Center.

3. The Alexandria Harmonizers went on to become the World Champion Barbershop Chorus not once but four times. They also got the visibility and respect they were looking for when the Kennedy Center itself invited the Harmonizers to perform as part of the nationally televised Kennedy Center Honors program when the Kennedy Center honored Irving Berlin in 1987. They sang "God Bless America."

4. Robert Aubry Davis and WETA-FM became so closely associated with the King's Singers that the station would eventually devote an entire evening during several of its pledge weeks in the mid-'80s to playing King's Singers recordings. They made more money for the station on those "King's Singers' Nights" than any other evening except for Saturday night and "Prairie Home Companion." When the King's Singers celebrated their 25th anniversary in Ann Arbor on May 2, 1993, at Hill Auditorium, Robert came from Washington, D.C., at my invitation to be the Master of Ceremonies for the concert.

5. The Levine School, started in 1976 by Diana Engel, Ruth Cogen, and Jackie Marlin, began as a community music school for kids that offered afterschool programs. Penny was one of its original faculty members and I was an early board member. The Levine School now has satellites throughout the Washington Metro Area serving people of all ages.

three
First Three Years at the Helm

I arrived in Ann Arbor on May 31, 1987, one day before I would start at the University Musical Society. Pulling in front of 1009 Berkshire Road, in one of the most beautiful residential neighborhoods of the city, I thought about the conspicuous rust on the side of my two-door Toyota Celica and the 140,000 miles on the odometer. I was alone in the car; for various reasons neither Matt nor Penny could join me until the end of the summer. Though I would be without their support for a while, I had the next best thing: the companionship of Jean Campbell. The spacious 1929 Tudor at 1009 Berkshire was hers, and I would be staying there for a couple of months, until Penny and Matt arrived and we found housing of our own.

Jean, the same age as my mom, was cofounder of the Center for the Education of Women at U-M and the widow of Angus Campbell, a cofounder of U-M's Institute for Social Research and longtime director of its Survey Research Center. Jean and I had met when I was in U-M grad school in the mid-1960s, just as she was launching the Center for the Education of Women, an organization that greatly interested those of us studying higher education. In addition, I had taken Angus Campbell's survey research course during the summer of 1967 and knew their daughter Joan Campbell, who was dating a friend at the time. I had kept in touch with Jean during my Washington years, in part because of our shared interests.

I discovered that having a person of the stature of Jean Campbell—who seemed to know everyone at the University of Michigan—as my friend, confidant, advisor, and companion for the first two months in Ann Arbor was a blessing beyond measure. For the next two months, as I tried to figure out what I was supposed to be doing, I would often return to Jean's home in the evenings and be greeted at the door with a suggestion that we sit in the kitchen or the back porch and discuss the day over a glass of wine.

I already knew a lot about the organization that I was going to be leading. Founded in 1879 and incorporated in 1880, the University Musical Society had a storied history as the oldest of the university-related presenting organizations. Furthermore, UMS's unique "independent, but deeply integrated" relationship with U-M served both UMS and U-M very well and was envied by other university presenters.

We were blessed with two venues that had long been favorites of the leading classical musicians: the 4,200-seat Hill Auditorium with its outstanding acoustics for orchestras and recitalists and the more intimate 1,100-seat Rackham Auditorium for chamber music. Hill had been opened in 1913 and Rackham in 1938. UMS had presented Vladimir Horowitz 15 times, the Chicago Symphony Orchestra 196 times, and the Philadelphia Orchestra 266 times. Many of the great classical solo artists and ensembles of the late 19th century and throughout the 20th century had made their way to Ann Arbor thanks to the artistic knowledge, personal relationships, negotiating skills, and pure determination of my five predecessors: Henry Simmons Frieze (1879–81, 1883–89), Alexander Winchell (1881–83, 1889–91), Francis Kelsey (1891–1927), Charles Sink (1927–57), and Gail Rector (1957–87).

On the morning of June 1, I drove to campus, parked, and walked to my office in Burton Memorial Tower, a campus landmark built in the 1930s as a memorial to Marion Leroy Burton, U-M president from 1920 to 1925. Because the UMS board had led an effort to raise funds from the Ann Arbor community toward the construction of the Tower, the organization was offered free office space on the first floor and in the basement of the building when it opened in 1936.

Sitting at my desk for the first time, I was surrounded by photos of the great artists who had appeared on the stages of the Hill and Rackham auditoria and the Power Center (a performance venue that opened in 1971). They all appeared to be gazing at me, reinforcing the feeling that all of the weight of the UMS tradition and legacy was now squarely on my shoulders. You have a reputation to maintain, they seemed to be saying, so don't mess it up.

Appreciative of that reminder of responsibility, I got to work learning the ins and outs of the job. I familiarized myself with each of the venues. I drove to Madison, Wisconsin, later in June with several staff members to attend the annual Big Ten presenters' conference and met my counterparts from these Midwest universities for the first time. I had breakfast and lunch with community leaders I'd met the previous spring, including Ann Arbor superintendent of schools Dick Benjamin, financial advisor Griff McDonald, and local developer Peter Allen.

I had great respect for those who had come before me and what they had done, but soon after assuming my duties, a great deal of my creative energy went to imagining what I could do differently, how I could build and improve on the UMS legacy.

The Burton Memorial Tower itself seemed to symbolize the situation. It represented for me many of the negative connotations of the phrase "ivory tower." I had a sense that, "stuck" in the tower, we were also stuck in an outmoded and tradition-bound way of doing things. UMS had always played it quite safe by sticking mostly to the classical music canon, presenting renowned orchestras, recitalists, chamber ensembles, and our own Choral Union. Also as a matter of tradition, the organization had very much of a top-down work culture. My two immediate predecessors, Charles Sink and Gail Rector, had made all key decisions about programming, marketing, and finances. There were no regular staff meetings nor did staff members have much of an opportunity to weigh in on key decisions. That's the way it was at UMS and at many other presenting organizations. Reinforcing the focus on executive authority, the president of UMS had also served as chair of the board of directors. (Fortunately, after they hired me, the board realized these two jobs needed to be separated; staff leadership and organizational governance shouldn't be the responsibility of the same person.)

The financial status of the organization also indicated that I needed to take a hard look at how we operated. One of the unavoidable facts staring at me as I assumed the role of president of UMS was that the organization carried a sizable debt. I came to understand that Gail Rector had been cautious about applying for financial support from government agencies or foundations. He was concerned about any "strings attached" that might somehow impact the quality of UMS's programming. There was some, but not much, corporate support. The members of the UMS board had also not been very engaged with fundraising. The development director's approach was to rely almost exclusively on individual support from a rela-tively small group of donors.

Although everyone was concerned about straightening out UMS's finances, many board members wanted to focus on controlling expenses. I wanted the same amount of emphasis placed on generating more revenue. This was where I saw an opportunity to make a difference. My main inter-est was in growing the organization by promoting it and raising money for its work. Those were my strengths—marketing and fundraising. That's what I had done in Washington, D.C., as a board member at the Levine School and Washington Bach Consort, as the managing director of Music at Noon, and with my Kennedy Center performances.

I knew intuitively, and from abundant experience, that the secret for success for any organization operating in the public sphere was connect-ing with people. An organization needs to be valued by the people who make up the community of which it is a part. You want people to feel that the organization's success is their success, their business. This means you must make it a priority to establish and nurture relationships with people, community organizations, businesses, and local leaders.

This philosophy was part of what I had learned from my mentor Pat-rick Hayes. His policy of "Everybody In, Nobody Out" arose from his commitment to collaboration—working with other groups with diverse missions and backgrounds. It was about making connections and forming partnerships for everyone's enrichment. The great thing about collabora-tion was that it could be the foundation of everything we needed to do as an organization: secure outside sources of funding, raise our visibility in the community, expand our audience, gain new insights, and build enthu-siasm for working on new projects.

As I looked around at the community, I saw that there were many local arts groups and various community-based cultural organizations with whom we had no significant relationship. They were natural collaborators because of our obvious shared interests. In addition, UMS had few mean-ingful connections with area businesses and media outlets, and virtually none with K-12 educational institutions and with nonprofits with missions outside the arts. The organization's "go-it-alone" approach had left it iso-lated and therefore vulnerable. I realized there were a whole host of ben-efits we stood to reap if we got unstuck and started to form connections.

A good first step, I thought, would be to practice a key idea outlined by Tom Peters and Robert Waterman in their 1982 book *In Search of*

Excellence—something they called "management by walking around." I needed to leave the office, meet people, show up at community events. I had begun to do this even before my official duties began in June: I attended some meetings of a group called Ann Arbor Area 2000 that included community leaders from different sectors of the city. It was a great way to meet Ann Arbor leaders and to let them know of my interest in engaging in the affairs of the community. Once I started the job, I also became engaged in Leadership Ann Arbor, a leadership development program sponsored by the Ann Arbor Chamber of Commerce that hosted monthly programs that connected me with leaders in business, government, education, and the nonprofit community.

I also saw the importance of connecting people within our own organization. We needed to change the organizational culture of UMS into something more collaborative and inclusive. Initiating dialogue with every member of the UMS staff was one of the things I set out to do right away. I met individually with each person to get to know them and what they did in their job. Aware that any inkling of future change could make some people anxious—and knowing I would depend on the knowledge and experience of seasoned staff members—I made it clear to each individual that I wasn't out to "clean house." But I also told people I would eventually be taking a hard look at how each staff member fit with the changes I was envisioning for the organization. As I got more comfortable in the job, I met again with each member of the staff. Together we looked six months out. We set forth a plan that included their ideas and mine and agreed that we would check back six months later.

As a relative newcomer to the field of presenting, I needed both to learn the ropes and to begin to build the professional network I knew I would need. So before the end of my first semester at UMS I'd made a point of attending the conferences of four different performing arts presenting organizations: Arts Midwest, the Association for Performing Arts Presenters (now the Association for Performing Arts Professionals—APAP in either case), the International Society for Performing Arts, and Chamber Music America. Thereafter, I continued to go to as many of these conferences as possible.

I found it revealing that very few of the leading presenters I met at professional conferences seemed to be all that impressed by UMS having presented the biggest names in the classical music world. They saw that we'd been around for a long time, had some fine venues, and were

part of a major university. In their view, we represented the staid, traditional mainstream of arts presentation. I'd introduce myself as the new
guy from Michigan and they'd ask, "What are you doing that's *interesting*?" With time, I realized they wanted to know what new works we
were commissioning, how we were approaching education, how we were
diversifying our programming, how we were engaging our community
and broadening our audiences. It felt awkward not to have much to
report along these lines.

But I was eager to learn from the experiences and perspectives of my
more seasoned colleagues. At each conference I attended the first year, I
randomly asked people who they considered to be the top presenters in the
country. After posing this question to more than 50 people, I developed
a good list of people considered the best by their peers. I then sought out
the 17 or so people whose names were repeatedly mentioned, hoping they
might become my friends and mentors. In this way I would learn from the
best in the field. Among these people were Ruth Felt at San Francisco Performances, Terre Jones at the Krannert Center at the University of Illinois,
Jackie Davis at the University of Kansas in Lawrence, Pebbles Wadsworth
at UCLA, Mikki Shepard at 651 ARTS in Brooklyn, and Susie Farr, who
had been a presenter at Stanford and UC Berkeley and had recently been
named the new executive director of the Association for Performing Arts
Presenters, our national association.

I found that when I asked these folks questions about how I should
do things, more often than not they'd respond by saying that, because
every community is different, they couldn't give me any specific formu-
las. In contrast, I learned the most from the questions they asked me—
particularly questions about how we defined our community and how well
we served it. I realized that since we were in the business of lifting up and
celebrating cultural expressions, we needed to know much more about the
cultural groups in our own backyard and what gifts they could be offering
us. We had a long way to go in accomplishing this goal, but we could get
there if we pointed ourselves in the right direction and dared to journey
further out of our tower.

During my first year or so at the job, I had ample opportunities to put into
practice new ideas for how UMS could carry out its mission. Even though
Gail Rector had booked performers for the 1987–88 season, I could design
and implement plans for marketing those performances to the public,

paying for them, and using them to better connect the town and gown communities with musical performance and our organization.

First on my agenda was working on the following spring's Ann Arbor May Festival. Presented by UMS since 1894, the festival was an annual affair during which a guest orchestra would come to Ann Arbor and perform up to six concerts in four days during the month of May (or late April). Leading vocal and instrumental soloists would be guest artists, and the UMS Choral Union, the town-gown chorus overseen by UMS, would always perform a great oratorio with the guest orchestra. For nearly the whole of the festival's history, a relationship had been established with a particular orchestra that came back year after year. The role of guest orchestra was filled for 11 years (1894–1904) by the Boston Festival Orchestra, for 31 years (1905–35) by the Chicago Symphony Orchestra, and for 49 years (1936–84) by the Philadelphia Orchestra.

By 1987, the May Festival faced several challenges. After Riccardo Muti took over as the new conductor of the Philadelphia Orchestra in 1980 he decided to end the orchestra's long-standing participation in the festival. The 1984 festival had been the Philadelphia Orchestra's last, and since then UMS had been unable to build a long-term, direct relationship with a single orchestra. The Pittsburgh Symphony Orchestra had been the guest orchestra in 1985 and 1986, and the Leipzig Gewandhaus Orchestra had served ably in that capacity in 1987. These were fine orchestras for the Festival, but their relationships with UMS were short-term. Their stop in Ann Arbor was one of several on a tour. There was limited repertoire to choose from and the soloists were already selected for the tour. And we had to deal with an agent, not directly with the orchestra, as had been the case with the earlier May Festival orchestras.

The May Festival also faced declining attendance. Because the academic year ended in late April, the Festival was held after classes had ended and most students had left campus. We couldn't draw on them as attendees. In addition, members of the local community and the region had more arts and culture choices available than ever before; this was a good thing, but it meant we had more competition.

For these reasons, the festival had become a money-losing operation. For many of the fiscal years since 1984, UMS had shown a positive bottom line for the regular season, lost money on the May Festival, and ended up with a loss for the year. That was a major downer for the staff.

It was therefore very important to see what we could do about rais-

Ken's first May Festival in 1988 featuring piano soloist Vladimir Feltsman (next to Ken) and the Pittsburgh Symphony with the conductor Michael Tilson Thomas (next to Feltsman). Joining the artists, each making his UMS debut, are Penny, Ken's mother Beth Fischer, and son Matt.

ing money for the 1988 Ann Arbor May Festival. I didn't want to undertake any major changes in the May Festival itself—and Gail had already booked the Pittsburgh Symphony Orchestra with Michael Tilson Thomas conducting, and virtually all of the programming except for the opening night soloist was already confirmed—but I had free rein in the areas of marketing and fundraising. Was there something that could be done with this May Festival that hadn't been done before and that might serve to bring in more people and improve the financial picture?

As a few staff and board colleagues joined me in thinking about approaches to fundraising for the festival, the theme of "marriage of old and new" occurred to us. This was reflected in the fact that the 1988 festival was a transition festival between the tenures of two UMS presidents, but in fundraising it suggested that in addition to involving established donors we could recruit new ones. We came up with the idea of finding four "new" families with philanthropic potential who could join four established donors as underwriters of the festival. We thought it would signal to the community that there was an emerging group of community leaders who might be willing to step up as patrons of the arts as the older families moved on.

Before putting this plan into action—we figured that it would be ideal to approach our potential underwriters about six or seven months prior to the festival—I had to devote my attention to the first performances of my tenure that would take place in the 4,200-seat Hill Auditorium. They were back-to-back performances of the Vienna Philharmonic, with Leonard Bernstein conducting, on September 21 and 22. Talk about intimidating.

The stakes were high for me. While I had not programmed these concerts, I knew that Bernstein would be choosing a handful of cities to take part in a North American tour already being planned in honor of his 70th birthday in 1988, a year later. When he came to Ann Arbor under UMS auspices, it would be my job to convince him that Ann Arbor should be one of the cities on next season's North American tour. It was a big deal for us: in addition to being Bernstein's 70th birthday it would also be the 75th anniversary of Hill Auditorium and we wanted to celebrate both occasions in one concert. I was aware that it would be a short tour and that many cities were bidding on the opportunity. I was the new guy. I had never met Bernstein—the great composer and conductor, a friend of presidents, the man whose *Mass*, commissioned by Jacqueline Kennedy, opened the Kennedy Center in 1971. What do I say? When do I ask him? Hoping Patrick Hayes could help get me through this extraordinary opportunity without my blowing it, I invited Patrick and his wife, Evelyn, to join Penny and me for the two performances.

The first night's performance was splendid. Bernstein gave us two audience favorites—Mozart's Clarinet Concerto in A Major featuring Peter Schmidl, first solo clarinetist in the Vienna Philharmonic, followed by Mahler's Symphony No. 5 with its beautiful Adagietto, which Bernstein had chosen to be performed at Robert Kennedy's funeral mass in 1968. The second night featured Mozart's Symphony no. 29, Bernstein's own Symphony No. 1, and Sibelius's Symphony no. 5. After the second concert was over, around 10:00 p.m., Bernstein proceeded to fulfill a commitment that was one of the things I loved about him: to greet every single person who stood in line to see him. It was about midnight when he greeted the last person in the line. I asked Patrick Hayes, who was with me backstage, if he'd like to join me in Bernstein's dressing room. Patrick, knowing the request I needed to make of Bernstein, told me he was not needed and assured me that I would do just fine on my own.

After the final of two concerts of the Vienna Philharmonic in September 1987, the first Hill Auditorium concerts of Ken's career at UMS, Ken got on his knee to invite conductor Leonard Bernstein to return to Ann Arbor the following year to celebrate Bernstein's 70th birthday and Hill Auditorium's 75th anniversary.

When Bernstein invited me into the conductor's dressing room, he had taken a shower, donned his bathrobe, and taken the one chair in the room. He had a scotch in one hand and a cigarette in the other. It was finally my chance to be alone with him and make my pitch.

Unable to sit and aware that standing over Bernstein was not the best way to make my pitch, I got down on my right knee and looked him in the eye. Without much in the way of preamble, I invited him to return in 1988. He responded in these exact words: "I love this town, I love the people of this town, and I love this hall. We'll be back." A few weeks later, he chose New York's Carnegie Hall, Washington's Kennedy Center, Toronto's Roy Thomson Hall, and Ann Arbor's Hill Auditorium as the stops on his birthday tour. Ann Arbor would be first. The concert was scheduled for October 29, 1988.

That fall, after the Vienna Philharmonic concerts, I returned to the task of recruiting our May Festival underwriters. Key board members and I identified potential donors. Then we visited with each family and made the request that each help cover the artist fees and major production costs. The whole plan depended on having eight donors, four established patrons and four emerging.

By early December, seven of the eight donors had confirmed. The *Ann Arbor News* was preparing to do a full-page story on this first-ever funding of the May Festival, the "marriage of old and new" theme, and the lineup for the Festival itself. It would be the first announcement of the opening-night soloist, pianist Vladimir Feltsman, a Russian émigré whose first concert in the United States had been at the Reagan White House a few months before. The story would be in the Sunday Arts section, which went to print on the previous Wednesday at noon. At 11:50 a.m. that Wednesday, I made a call in the lobby of Carnegie Hall, where I was attending the 1987 International Society for Performing Arts conference, to the eighth and final donor, who had asked for more time. I needed his commitment and I got it! I immediately called the *Ann Arbor News*; the heartwarming article appeared in that Sunday's paper.

When we started work on the 1988 May Festival program book, we composed a fitting acknowledgment of the underwriters' generosity:

> Bravo to May Festival Underwriters. In the spirit of honoring the past and ensuring the future, these families and individuals have demonstrated their support by underwriting the artist fees and major production costs of this 95th Annual May Festival. Representing both long-time Ann Arbor arts patrons and a new generation of leadership in the cultural life of this community, these donors are committed to maintaining the Musical Society's tradition of excellence through their public-spirited generosity. We gratefully recognize the following: Dennis A. Dahlmann, Mrs. Theophile Raphael, Elizabeth E. Kennedy, Mr. and Mrs. Peter N. Heydon, Eileen and Ron Weiser with McKinley Associates, Inc., Bill and Sally Martin, An anonymous family, and The Power Foundation.

To afford the 1988 Leonard Bernstein concert and cover all our expenses, we had to have income in excess of $200,000. If we could raise approximately half this amount from the local business community, we'd be in good shape. With that in mind, we started developing ideas for what would become our critically important corporate sponsorship program.

Great Lakers Bancorp was the sponsor of the three December 1988 Messiah performances -- "A Harmonious Community Endeavor" -- that brought together the UMS Choral Union under conductor Donald Bryant, the Ann Arbor Symphony Orchestra, and four soloists, from left, soprano Ashley Putnam, mezzo-soprano Kathleen Segar, tenor Richard Fracker, and bass-baritone Stephen Bryant -- all alumni of the U-M School of Music.

It was an ambitious plan that would require us to establish new relationships with businesses that had little or no previous involvement with us. Before focusing on getting sponsors for the Bernstein concert in the fall, however, I could try my hand at getting a sponsor for an event with lower costs, where the stakes weren't quite so high. Every year on the first weekend in December, UMS presented Handel's *Messiah* featuring the UMS Choral Union, a contracted orchestra, and professional soloists. Corporate sponsorship of that event would contribute significantly to our bottom line.

My target was Great Lakes Bancorp, a medium-sized regional bank that had no previous relationship with UMS. Before going to see Roy Weber, its president, I called my brother Jerry, who was a vice president and chief financial officer of what is now US Bank in Minnesota, to ask for advice. "First thing, little brother," he said, "don't try to sell him on UMS. I know you well. That's your instinct—to sell. Rather, go in there, ask questions, and listen to the answers. Let him talk. By doing so you'll receive clues on what really matters to him." What great advice that was! When I sat down in front of Mr. Weber's desk, I said simply, "Mr. Weber, tell me about your bank." He was eager to tell me a great deal. He had great pride in the bank, which was (at that time) the only locally owned and locally headquartered bank in Ann Arbor. And it had been around for a long time.

Then I asked him what organizations he supported. He was pleased to recognize them. In his list were the Ann Arbor Symphony and the University of Michigan. These were key facts. When he asked me, "What can I do for you, Ken?," I knew what to say. "Mr. Weber, you know the oldest thing we do at UMS is Handel's *Messiah.* Like your bank, UMS and the *Messiah* have been around for a long time. Furthermore, this year's *Messiah* features the Ann Arbor Symphony, and all the soloists have studied at the U-M School of Music. With all these local connections, I'd like to offer Great Lakes the opportunity to be this year's *Messiah* sponsor." He smiled and looked receptive, so I continued. "Mr. Weber, for a $10,000 gift, this is what happens. That check comes to UMS, but it stays with UMS for only a short time, because we'll use that money to pay the fee of the Ann Arbor Symphony. The Ann Arbor Symphony will then distribute it to each of its members. Do you know what they're going to do with their money, Mr. Weber? Put it back in your bank. So imagine, Mr. Weber, all the good that your $10,000 will do as it makes its way around the community before coming back to you." Sold on the idea right away, he wrote a check for $10,000. The important lesson from this experience was that it was important to find out what matters to a person before you ask them for money. From that point forward, I understood that a relationship with a corporation had to be seen as a partnership in which we helped one another achieve our objectives.

My successful encounter with Mr. Weber gave me confidence as we moved forward with our plan to secure corporate sponsors for the upcoming Leonard Bernstein concert. Several months before the concert, we reserved Hill Auditorium for five afternoons during the week. Each day about two dozen business leaders plus their spouses would gather backstage. We then invited them to come to the Hill Auditorium stage, which was set up in the form of an orchestra. On each music stand was a flyer with details about the concert. Board member Norm Herbert greeted them, and then he took his seat where the concertmaster would normally sit in the violin section. Then I came out in tails and, like the conductor would, stood on the podium. I told the assembled business leaders—now aware of their metaphorical role as the orchestra—about the historic nature of the Bernstein concert, noting that it would be the conductor's 70th birthday and Hill Auditorium's 75th anniversary. I added that Ann Arbor was one of only four North American cities to have the honor of being on the tour. Then I asked each person to look out into the auditorium. I told them not one seat had yet been claimed (the first day, anyway). I then asked them to close their eyes.

After a short stretch of silence, a recording of the dramatic opening of the third movement of Brahms's Fourth Symphony, with Bernstein conducting the Vienna Philharmonic, blasted from the sound system. We listened for about 20 seconds. I told the group as they opened their eyes, "What you just heard will be performed live on this stage by the same orchestra led by the same conductor. You do not want to miss this event. Now, look out into the audience, and let me know which of these 4,200 seats you want UMS to reserve for your business." The first time we did this, Ron Weiser, chair of McKinley Associates, stood up and pronounced, "I want those forty right there," pointing to some great seats on the main floor. Following Ron's cue, a handful of other executives each claimed their share of seats. We had similar results each day. In the end, 42 companies purchased more than 850 tickets. With all of those tickets priced at $125, we had exceeded our sponsorship goal. Perhaps more importantly, we had primed local businesses and corporations to see how their companies could use a performing arts event to accomplish objectives like customer appreciation, client cultivation, employee reward, and corporate visibility.

To raise the other half of the needed funding, the UMS Advisory Committee, a group of volunteers who were assisting UMS mainly by organizing social events related to UMS performances, proposed having individual patrons buy tickets at the same level—$125 each—as part of a special package that would include dinner and transportation to the concert. You would drive your car to the home of a UMS volunteer, eat dinner there, then board a university bus that would drop you off in front of the Hill Auditorium so you wouldn't have to worry about parking. After enjoying the fabulous concert, you'd find your bus and return to the host's home for cordials and dessert. We were thrilled that over 850 people purchased tickets at this level.

We had found a way to engage the corporate community to support the concert and had a way for the general public to be involved as well. Our next question: How could we assure that students would be able to see and hear this great orchestra and conductor?

We knew that Bernstein would love to see young people in the hall, so for the 1988 concert we made a special effort to maximize the involvement of the students. In the spirit of "Everybody In, Nobody Out," we set aside 550 tickets to be sold to students for $10 each. Then another opportunity was dropped in our laps. Earlier in the year the U-M Regents had named a new president of the University, James J. Duderstadt, whose tenure would begin on October 1, four weeks before the concert. I went to Jim and his wife, Anne, and proposed that they host a postperformance reception in their home for Bernstein, noting that it would be a big hit with major donors. Jim and Anne said they would think about it and came back with this idea: instead of inviting major donors, let's invite a group of about 30 U-M students, young conductors, composers, and pianists, who were doing now what Bernstein might have been doing at their age. I thought it was brilliant.

Now that the new president had committed to hosting Bernstein with a group of students, I needed to figure out how to guarantee that Bernstein would attend the event. He was well known for enjoying postperformance parties with associates and friends that would go well into the early morning hours. How could I make sure that he would attend a party at the president's home with 30 U-M students instead of some other gathering?

I hadn't yet figured out the best strategy when we informed the student body that the UMS box office at Burton Tower would open at 9:00 a.m. on a Saturday morning a few weeks before the concert for the significantly discounted student tickets. The first of the students arrived 14 hours in advance, all bundled up, and sat outside Burton Memorial Tower all night. The students' interest was contagious and infused a lot of energy into the staff. At 6:00 a.m. the next morning, UMS staff members and I arrived with orange juice and donut holes. The line had grown to more than 400.[1]

The idea occurred to us that if Bernstein were aware that there were hundreds of students waiting in line, some for 14 hours, for the opportunity to see him conduct, he might commit to the party at the president's home.

Students turned out in huge numbers to purchase specially priced student tickets for the October 29, 1988 concert featuring Leonard Bernstein and the Vienna Philharmonic commemorating Bernstein's 70th birthday and Hill Auditorium's 75th anniversary.

My colleagues and I started a clipboard at each end of the line, and on that clipboard was a little piece of masking tape that read, "Send a message to Lenny." While the clipboards were being passed along, I got the names and contact information for the first ten students in the line, thinking that I'd invite them to the party at President Duderstadt's if we got Bernstein to commit.

With three hours to kill, the queued-up students had plenty of time to compose creative messages:

> Dear Mr. B., my mom and dad fell in love listening to *West Side Story* and I'm the product. If I'm not in this line, my ass is grass.
> —Joey, class of '91

> Hey, Lenny, you've written concertos for everybody else. How 'bout me?
> —Eddie, bassoon major, Class of '89

We made four copies of the 100 or so "messages to Lenny" along with a set of photos that I took that morning. I mailed packets to Bernstein's manager, Harry Kraut; his publicist, Maggie Carson; Columbia Artists' agent David Foster; and an official with the Vienna Philharmonic. My cover letter said something to this effect: "Dear Mr. Bernstein. These messages and photos come from the next generation of your fans. Some have spent the night in the chilly Michigan October, waiting in line for up to 14 hours for the opportunity to see you. How about coming to the U-M President James Duderstadt's home after the concert for a reception with some of these young people?" Within a short time I got a response that Bernstein would be there for sure. Music School dean Paul Boylan identified twenty music students to invite and I added the names of the first ten students in line I'd collected earlier. We gave this list to President Duderstadt's office, and he and Anne invited each student to their home after the performance to meet Leonard Bernstein.

We got local high school students involved in the concert as well. The Pioneer High School orchestra would be visiting Vienna on a European tour the next summer, so we knew these students and their parents would be enthusiastic about organizing an event during which they could connect with members of the Vienna Philharmonic Orchestra. On the night before the concert, the students and their families hosted a food court in the lobby of the Power Center, with food donated by local restaurants. Each family was paired with a member of the Vienna Philharmonic. A student quartet was performing when the Vienna Philharmonic president, cellist Werner Resel, suggested to the student cellist that they exchange places so the student could get something to eat. With Werner playing the student's cello, the quartet continued its performance. After the reception, the local families gave their guests three options: go to the Friday night Pioneer football game, attend the annual Bandorama concert at Hill Auditorium featuring U-M bands, or go out to dinner. The members of the orchestra seemed to enjoy the opportunity to connect with the young high school musicians, their families, and the local community.

On the Saturday afternoon of the Bernstein gala, a representative of the management company that was handling the Vienna Philharmonic tour stopped by our home. He commented that UMS seemed to enjoy doing a big performance like Bernstein's 70th birthday tour, and I concurred. He then asked if we would be interested in being involved in what he referred to as one of the management's next big projects. It was bringing the Metropolitan Opera Orchestra out of the pit and onto the stage. He men-

Bernstein holding court with 30 U-M students at a post-concert reception at the President's House hosted by James and Anne Duderstadt. Twenty of the students were conductors, composers, and pianists; the other ten were the first in line, some arriving 14 hours in advance, to purchase the specially priced student tickets.

tioned that James Levine, the Met's principal conductor, who would be conducting the orchestra on the tour, believed the Met Orchestra was the best in New York City and needed to be heard on stage. He was looking three years ahead to 1991. He asked if UMS would be interested and I said yes. That seed would later sprout and bear its fruit.

The Bernstein 70th birthday concert was spectacular, featuring Beethoven (Leonore Overture no. 3), Bernstein (Halil and Prelude, Fugue, and Riffs), and Brahms (Symphony no. 4). I was particularly gratified to see 550 students arrayed throughout the house in all sections. I knew we'd done something right when I saw a student in khakis and a sweater sitting next to a chief executive officer in a tux on the Main Floor. One paid $10, the other $125, and they were both having a grand time.

As the audience exited the hall after the concert, Pioneer orchestra members, distributed at each exit, handed each person a box containing

Following the sit-down conversation with the students, Bernstein went to the piano at 1:30 a.m. and regaled them with tunes from his *Candide* and *West Side Story*. He then invited the students to join him at the Full Moon bar in downtown Ann Arbor, reminding them to bring their IDs. They closed the Full Moon at 4:30 a.m..

a small piece of birthday cake. The printing on the box commemorated Bernstein's 70th birthday and Hill Auditorium's 75th anniversary.

The reception in the president's home after the concert was magical. For about an hour and a half, Leonard Bernstein held court with thirty U-M students, all in tuxes or suits and fancy dresses. At 1:30 a.m., Penny and I noticed that the Duderstadts were, like us, showing signs of fading. I went to Mr. Bernstein and said, "I think it's time to go." He said, "I don't think so," went to the piano, and started playing tunes from *West Side Story* and *Candide*. I could imagine being in the students' shoes. You're hanging out in the president's home talking with Leonard Bernstein, and suddenly this world-renowned conductor and composer plays those famous tunes just for you. Ten minutes later, Bernstein got up from the piano. "Okay, Ken," he asked, "now where's that place you told me we can go from here?"

I told him it was the Full Moon, a downtown bar, the manager of which had said he'd stay open as long as Bernstein wanted to be there and as long as each student brought ID. Bernstein gathered everybody up and asked,

"Who has cars?" Some upperclassmen raised their hands. He told them to take as many as they could down to the Full Moon. He said that anyone without a ride could "come ride with me in the limo." He and the students didn't leave the Full Moon until about 4:30 a.m.

With the 1988 Bernstein concert we took big steps forward in community engagement and visibility, catalyzing what would be big changes in UMS. Despite the success of the event, however, the UMS board remained cautious. I was still the new kid who had to be watched. But it was becoming clearer to everyone that a policy of "Everybody In, Nobody Out," of widening the circle and bringing more people in, just made sense.

The year 1989 would prove to be another significant one for UMS. Between events and performances, additions to the staff, the initiation of new programs, and new efforts to get us connected to the community, much happened that would help move us forward.

An education program was one of the important results of the planning and meetings that occurred that year. It was Penny who had encouraged me, not long after I started as president of UMS, to think about creating a program that would engage kids with music. It was natural for Penny to ask, "What will UMS be doing to develop the next generation of audience members?" She began teaching flute when she was in high school, had taught every year since then, and was one of the original teachers at the Levine School of Music in Washington, D.C., in the mid-1970s. Her interest in engaging young people was shared by many of the other presenters I was talking with, so hers was not the only voice I heard on the subject.

When the time came that we could begin to think seriously about getting an education program started, sometime after the Bernstein concert in the fall of 1988, I wanted to be sure we first consulted with teachers, administrators, parents, music educators, and staff colleagues. I was determined that we would do enough listening and planning so that, whatever we did, we would have a good chance for success from the get-go. Of particular importance was anticipating every question or concern a teacher or parent would have that would stand in the way of success: bussing, cost, parental permission, timing, and so on. One early decision we made was that the program would not be free. There would need to be a cost so that it would be valued. The most important decision, however, was to seek the advice of Ann Arbor Public School's new music coordinator Deborah Katz in the late summer of 1989.

We went to her home at the top of a hill in Ann Arbor. I had a feeling we were going to the mountaintop to speak with a seer. When we entered Deb's home, she was sitting Buddha-style with an infant child in her lap. We told her about our intention to begin an education program for the Ann Arbor Public Schools and asked her what advice she had for us. "Begin with opera," she said after a moment, looking down from her perch on the couch. "Invite every fourth grader in Ann Arbor to come to the Power Center to see opera. In the third grade, it's too early. By fifth grade, it's too late. Fourth graders will eat it up. Opera has music, theater, dance, story. You can abbreviate the performance to an hour, but don't dumb it down. If the opera is in Italian or French or German, use surtitles."

We did exactly what Deb Katz told us to do. Planning proceeded apace, with many people contributing their time, energy, and ideas. By February 1990 we were ready to launch the program. The New York City Opera National Company came to Ann Arbor with Puccini's *La Bohème* and put on two abbreviated one-hour daytime programs for the fourth graders on Friday, February 16, and then did the complete opera, once on Saturday evening the 17th and twice on Sunday the 18th, for regular audiences. We charged $5 per student. It was so successful that it earned us the Dawson Award for Distinctive Programming at the 1990 December Arts Professionals conference.

The concept of partnership, which we had been using to direct our fundraising, was realized in the area of event presentation in a particularly significant way when we partnered with the U-M School of Music to copresent the Michigan MozartFest during a four-day period, November 16–19, 1989.

The idea for the event came from the fertile minds of pianist Penny Crawford and her husband, music historian Richard Crawford, both on the U-M faculty. Rich and Penny's original conception was for an extravaganza that would include all 23 of Mozart's piano concertos, performed by a roster of fortepianists with an orchestra of period instruments. They soon scaled down that notion, not for lack of fortepianists but because the task lay beyond the orchestral resources we could muster. Plus, it would take a long time to do that many concertos.

We planned the event over a series of delicious and lively dinners during 1988 and early 1989 at the Crawford home on Baldwin Avenue, with a flip chart ready at a corner of the table to record our many ideas. The new formula we settled on was to present nine of Mozart's piano concerti with ten outstanding fortepianists (one concerto would be the double concerto). They would perform with the local period instrument ensemble Arts Musica. There would be an artistic director/conductor working with Penny Crawford who would be able to turn back the clock to conduct the historically informed performances. A respected Mozart scholar would work with Richard Crawford to design a set of daytime seminars on the subject featuring leading Mozart scholars from around the world. Both the concerts and scholarly programs would be held at the Rackham Building on the U-M campus (we were able to obtain this venue only with the cooperation of Saul Hymans, who graciously moved the high-profile annual Economic Outlook Conference, always held on those same days at Rackham, to North Campus).

We invited Roger Norrington to be the conductor and Mozart scholar Neal Zaslaw to be the seminar director. We had wonderful volunteer help from Shelly Williams. Our friends at Amadeus Café in downtown Ann Arbor agreed to set up a small café in the lobby of the Rackham Building so that concertgoers could have snacks and beverages at intermission. Thanks to Larry Weis, a friend in public relations at Ford Motor Company, we obtained a generous sponsorship from Ford Motor Company that included brand-new cars for the media to use during the festival. Ford's sponsorship would also enable us to record the concerts and make them available for delayed broadcast. The School of Music received a grant from the National Endowment for the Humanities to offset expenses for the scholarly sessions.

We wanted to generate interest in the arts press well before the MozartFest event, but we needed a hook. Word was leaking out about the ambitious Lincoln Center Mozart Project that would be carried out over two seasons in 1991 and 1992 to commemorate the 200th anniversary of Mozart's death. The ambition was to have the partners of Lincoln Center— opera, orchestra, chamber music, Juilliard, and so forth—perform all of Mozart's 835 works during this time frame. With such a huge undertaking happening in New York City, how could we get the press interested in our important, but much more modest, Michigan MozartFest?

We came up with the idea of hosting a press luncheon in a place in New York where most of the music writers had never been but had always been curious about. That place was the 1901 New York Yacht Club on W. 44th Street. Ann Arbor's Bill Martin, who had helped support the 1988 Ann Arbor May Festival and just happened to be president of the U.S. Sailing Association and a member of the Yacht Club, helped us obtain access to one of the rooms adjacent to the Yacht Club's splendid Model Room. The Model Room is a huge, two-story room with a Tiffany ceiling in which are displayed intricate models of yachts from all over the world, including fully rigged models of America's Cup winners dating back to 1870. With our luncheon in the adjacent room, the members of the New York press who attended the press luncheon would be able to experience the Model Room both on the way in and the way out. It worked. We got 14 reporters and writers to attend, pitched our Michigan MozartFest as a prelude to the larger event happening later in New York, and received some good press coverage both before and after our festival.

The MozartFest itself went off splendidly. Roger Norrington encouraged the audience members to imagine they were in a concert hall at the time Mozart wrote most of the concertos (the mid-1780s) and to feel free to abandon the conventional concert etiquette of the present day. If you felt like clapping after a brilliant cadenza or between movements, he said, do so. Lighten up. Enjoy. Have fun. And we did.

It was during 1989 that our goal of collaborating with other organizations yielded results in the field of composition. In December of 1987, Doug Wheeler, of Washington Performing Arts, had convened a group of six of us presenters at the International Society for Performing Arts conference. We discussed informally how we could introduce new works into the concert scene, particularly for the recital repertoire. Our idea was for our several organizations to share the cost of commissioning the new works, making it more affordable. And then we could each present the work, assuring that it would be heard. Our informal group approached the cellist Yo-Yo Ma as an artist who might like to have a piece written for him to perform. His enthusiasm for the idea led us to composer William Bolcom, a recently named Pulitzer Prize winner and U-M faculty member. He accepted the commission and set about writing a composition for Yo-Yo Ma and Emanuel Ax, completing his Sonata for Cello and Piano in 1989.[2] Thus began UMS's engagement in co-commissioning new work. We had high hopes for this strategy, and in future years it would indeed bring amazing results and lead us down extraordinarily productive paths that dovetailed with other goals.

During the first three years or so of my tenure, I was able to hire a number of staff members to replace those who retired or left for other reasons or where it was clear we needed their expertise. When a position opened up, I set about trying to identify people who were competent but also believed that we could be making decisions together. Some extraordinary people came our way, often at just the right time. By early 1990, we had in place a team that would prove to be crucial in shaping UMS's future.

In 1987, a student in his early twenties, Michael Kondziolka, came to Michigan from Saint Olaf College to begin work on a master's in clarinet performance. He became a UMS intern that year, seeking experiences in every part of UMS—ticket office, marketing, development, production. I observed that he had knowledge of and passion for the arts in addition to good administrative and negotiating skills. He had worked in financial services after his undergraduate degree and had been an Arthur Murray dance instructor before coming to U-M. After his internship was over, in early September 1988, I hired Michael to continue working as an assistant in the many areas where he served as an intern. He would become UMS's programming director in the early 1990s.[3]

In 1988, an 18-year-old second-year student named Sara Billmann joined us as a work-study student, working in our marketing department with marketing director Robin Stephenson. She was at the music school studying oboe, but soon shifted to liberal arts, dropped the oboe, and became an English major. Sara was bright and had a facility with numbers and writing. She joined the full-time UMS staff after she graduated in 1990. She would soon become associate director of marketing and manager of the UMS Choral Union, in addition to assisting with our emerging education program.[4]

In 1989 I was able to hire John B. Kennard Jr. from the U-M health system to join us as our first full-time finance director. He was the single parent of an adopted five-year-old boy named Tony. At the health system John had not found the flexibility he needed to spend time with his son. Although John was far more qualified and had far more experience than we needed at the time, John took the job—along with a significant salary cut. John's only requests were that he be able to attend his son's activities and that I would seek to narrow the gap in his salary over time. As a father who took an active role in my own son's upbringing, I greatly admired John's decision to put his family first. As finance director, John was able to clean up our serious financial mess within a few months.[5]

Within about a year of my taking on the job of UMS president, everyone recognized that we needed additional financial resources. Expanding and diversifying our programming would require more money, and much of what we were contemplating—such as having artists spend more time in our community for master classes, class visits, school-day performances, and so on—would generate little or no income. It was clear we needed someone who could work full time at fundraising and donor development. So in 1989 I hired Catherine Arcure from Washtenaw Community College as our new development director. She had experience in every kind of fundraising: corporate giving and sponsorship, government and foundation grants, planned giving by individuals, solicitation of major gifts, and annual giving.

In addition to these new folks, two seasoned veterans—box office manager Michael Gowing and administrative assistant Sally Cushing—stayed on through the period of change that accompanied my arrival (and, it would turn out, well beyond that). Everyone felt grateful for their accumulated knowledge and experience and the continuity they represented.

During the 1989–90 academic year, once both John Kennard and Cathy Arcure were on board, we began convening meetings every Tuesday morning of all the people at UMS in management positions. We began calling ourselves the M-Team. We discussed all matters of concern to the organization, from administrative procedures to long-term planning and strategizing. Everyone's voice mattered. There was mutual respect for each person's role, and anyone was welcome to comment on anything that came up. No major decision was made without the ins and outs of its consequences and opportunities being discussed extensively at our meetings.

The M-Team was the realization of the more collaborative, team-based approach that I had sought from the beginning. I was thrilled to have talented, dedicated people with whom I could lead UMS into the future. I had the sense, too, that as long as I treated these key members of the staff—and everyone in the organization, for that matter—with respect and admiration, and appreciated that they knew far more than I did in their areas of expertise, they would be around for a long time.

Notes

1. Over 20 years later, I became reacquainted with the first-year student who was first in line that cold evening in October. I had a photo of her wrapped in a blanket outside Burton Tower, but I didn't know who she was until a mutual friend connected us. She was Jennifer Dautermann, the cofounder of Classical:NEXT, head-

quartered in Berlin, which hosts one of the world's most important classical music meetings. Jennifer told me when we finally met: "That night was a true inspiration for me."

2. The work received its Ann Arbor premiere on December 10, 1991, in Hill Auditorium and is now part of the standard cello repertoire.

3. Michael Kondziolka is today one of the most admired and respected programming directors on the international arts scene.

4. After receiving an MBA from Stanford in 1995 and working for a year as a financial analyst at the San Francisco Opera, Sara returned to UMS as our director of marketing in August 1996. She has become a leading marketing and communications professional and a sought-after consultant and speaker on marketing and audience research.

5. John developed financial principles and practices for UMS that worked exceptionally well for us. He shared these freely with financial officers at other university-related and stand-alone presenting organizations, garnering him enormous admiration and respect from the field. He also had the admiration and respect of the members of the U-M financial operations staff and the UMS board, among whom were seasoned financial professionals eager to assure that UMS would always be a fiscally responsible organization. Sadly, John died from cancer six months after I retired, just short of his 65th birthday.

four
Out of the Tower

Around the third anniversary of my tenure as president of UMS, in early June 1990, I began to feel that both the organization and I were ready to move ahead. In addition to meeting the needs and challenges that presented themselves, I had spent the previous three years learning, preparing, planning, laying foundations, dreaming—essentially laying out a path for the organization to follow—and now it seemed time to begin walking that path.

The participatory nature of the work I'd done designing conferences before coming to UMS had provided a natural tie to a performing arts organization that envisioned itself becoming more welcoming and inclusive, where we actively sought ways for a variety of people to become engaged through various points of entry. That general goal suddenly seemed all the more important—and focused itself more sharply—after I read a newly published book-length report put together by the National Task Force on Presenting and Touring the Performing Arts, chaired by Jerry Yoshitomi.

Entitled *An American Dialogue*, the 1989 report encouraged presenters to commission new work, take risks, develop educational programs, diversify programming and audiences, educate the next generation, become curators, and serve as community leaders. Emphasizing that presenters should be doing more than just arranging gigs and monitoring ticket sales, it advocated diversifying and being welcoming to everyone. The book was meant to stimulate presenters to think about what was possible in terms of engaging people from all parts of the community, and it had exactly that effect on me.

I was already aiming at connecting with other performing and visual arts organizations, educational institutions, local nonprofits, and area businesses. *An American Dialogue* convinced me that this wasn't enough, that we should be forming not just connections but true partnerships, relationships that garnered tangible benefits for both parties. Most importantly, it opened my eyes to the fact that our regional community of southeast Michigan consisted of many people whose skin color, spiritual beliefs and traditions, cultural backgrounds, and ethnic identities were different from those of most of my colleagues and friends. It was clear to me that UMS would need to engage these various communities and consider their different notions of art, culture, and music when we made our programming decisions.

It made sense for us to advance this broad and ambitious agenda incrementally, and with different goals addressed one by one. When we found out in 1989 that the Arts Partners Program of the Association of Performing Arts Presenters was soliciting proposals for grants related to partnerships with community arts organizations, we seized on the opportunity to better develop our ties with other groups in our larger community with related missions and shared goals.

We envisioned bringing an artist to campus for a three-week residency involving workshops, performances, and other collaborative activities. UMS would serve as the required university-affiliated sponsor for the project but would work in partnership with the local groups. It would be the first time, to my knowledge, that UMS had ever convened the local arts community to discuss a project of mutual benefit. We applied for and received a $3,400 planning grant from APAP, which was acting as the fiscal agent for funds provided by the Lila Wallace–Reader's Digest Fund.

To gather ideas for which artist to approach—and to bring in the project's first partner organization—I got together with Russ Collins, head of the Michigan Theater. I had a lot of respect for Russ, whom I met when I first arrived in 1987. His Michigan Theater was a refurbished 1928 vaudeville house with 1,700 seats that served as both a film and live performance venue. Russ was presenting artists like Laurie Anderson, Philip Glass, Bill T. Jones/Arnie Zane Dance Company, and Sankai Juku. Having just had André Previn in Ann Arbor, conducting the Los Angeles Philharmonic for the 1990 May Festival, I suggested that we bring in Previn to engage with local arts groups. Russ thought Previn would be a great choice. Prior to his most recent visit, between 1978 and 1987, Previn had conducted four

The Ann Arbor delegation meets with André Previn at his suburban New York home to discuss the Arts Partners Program. From left, André Previn, Ken Fischer, Russ Collins, and Ed Surovell.

concerts at Hill Auditorium, two with the London Symphony and one each with the Royal Philharmonic and Pittsburgh Symphony orchestras. I knew Previn had a great affection for Ann Arbor; he had once told me that Ann Arbor's Liberty Record Shop was the finest record store in the world. As a jazz pianist, chamber musician, conductor, and composer in many genres, including film scores (for which he received four Academy Awards), Previn was uniquely qualified to interact with a variety of arts organizations in our community. This was the main objective of the Arts Partners Program—identify an individual artist or producing organization that would come to a community and engage not only with the host presenter but also with other arts, educational, and community organizations.

Russ and I, representing the Michigan Theater and UMS, respectively, convened a group of local arts leaders, including representatives from the Ann Arbor Symphony, the Southeast Michigan Jazz Association, the University of Michigan School of Music, and the Kerrytown Concert House, to develop ideas for a residency with André Previn. We had in mind that Previn could conduct the Ann Arbor Symphony, work with composition students at the School of Music, play chamber music at Kerrytown, play jazz piano under the auspices of the Southeast Michigan Jazz Association at a local club, host a showing at the Michigan Theater of the four Academy Award–winning films that he had scored, and engage in other community events under UMS auspices.

The $3,400 planning grant enabled Russ and me, along with UMS board member and realtor Edward Surovell, to travel to New York in September 1990 and meet with Previn at his home in Bedford Hills north of New York City. Previn liked our ideas for the residency and indicated his readiness to come to Ann Arbor to meet with our larger group and begin planning the details. We scheduled that meeting for January 5, 1991.

Back in Ann Arbor, representatives from all the participating groups discussed what would happen when Previn came in January. We planned to host a reception at which we would introduce Previn and unveil our plans to our respective staffs and boards of directors. The members of our boards would meet Previn, learn how each organization would benefit from his presence in our community, and, we hoped, declare their support for the residency plan. Then UMS would apply for the maximum $150,000 grant to support the costs of the three-week project. The guidelines allowed for the artist to take up to two years to fulfill the three-week obligation. This kind of flexibility was particularly attractive to Previn, who had a very busy conducting and performing schedule. He was clearly committed to making the Ann Arbor project work, and we talked about launching it in February 1993.

Seeing the proposal as a slam dunk, I went ahead with the planning. Russ and I put together an invitation for the board members of the respective organizations to attend the reception in January, creating special letterhead displaying the logos of all the partner organizations. When UMS board members received the invitation, many expressed concern about what all of it meant. The notion of partnering with other groups in the community was new to UMS, and I had not brought the idea to the board for discussion. I had just moved forward, knowing that the Arts Partners Program, with its funding resources, was a win-win opportunity. The board, however, was anxious about our financial obligations. Yes, a grant *might* be good for UMS, but what risk might it entail? I was reminded that we were in debt to the University of Michigan. Then, Previn told us that because of an injury he would be unable to make the trip to Ann Arbor for the planning session or the reception. In the end, I was not permitted to submit a full proposal. Planning came to a halt and we called off the whole project.

I was disappointed, of course, and very much aware that the organization I led was letting down so many others. Rather than being terribly upset, however, I chose to own the problem. I recognized that I had failed on three accounts: I had not understood the depth of the board's financial concerns; I had not taken the time to educate the board about the value of collaboration as a win-win for all; and I had not explained why André Previn was the perfect Arts Partner for our community. In simple terms, I had failed to lead.

The whole affair was a significant embarrassment, but like many such things it was also an important learning experience. The main lesson I learned was that the CEO needs to take responsibility for educating the members of the board. I needed to take the time to talk to them, give them enough background, and assure good discussions. I couldn't assume that what was self-evidently positive to me appeared the same way to them. They would welcome good ideas and sound proposals but also wanted to know the why, the how, and the how much. Their concerns about the financial obligations were well founded—looking out for the organization's long-term fiscal health was, after all, one of their primary responsibilities. They were right that because of our debt to the university, every project we undertook had to be fiscally responsible. As a leader with strengths and experience in promotion and development—bringing money in—I needed to concern myself much more with monitoring and managing expenses. Making this shift in orientation made me a stronger, more well-rounded leader, better able to lead UMS down the path we envisioned.

About the same time that we were working on the Arts Partners project involving André Previn, UMS was making its first real efforts to promote diversity. Because *An American Dialogue* had sensitized me and others on the UMS staff to issues of cultural diversity, we began to understand that by unthinkingly embracing music and musicians in the European high cultural tradition as representative of "culture" and "the arts," we were perpetuating the dominance of that tradition and alienating people from other cultures and traditions and backgrounds. Looking at the faces of those on the staff and the board—and, to a great extent, of those in our audiences and on our stages—we realized that most were white and likely of northern European extraction. They were not representative of the community in our own backyard, which included large numbers of people who identified as Arab, African American, Mexican American, and Asian. We resolved to work toward changing this situation.

In 1990, we applied for and received a small "diversity" grant from the Lila Wallace–Reader's Digest Fund administered by Arts Presenters. We used these funds to engage Gwen Cochran Hadden, a diversity consultant. She spent the morning with the staff and the early afternoon with the board, and then gathered us all together in the late afternoon to share her observations and recommendations.

We expected a somewhat lengthy discourse. But Gwen was extraordinarily brief, basically telling us, "Start where you are." It was such a simple message that we struggled to understand what it meant. Our first inclination had been to look outside our organization to find the most prominent, most respected black people in town and invite them to become involved with UMS. But Gwen set us on a better course. She said that "starting where we are" would mean looking deep within our own organization to find people we had overlooked or ignored who would welcome an invitation to become more involved.

Sure enough, such people existed. Taking Gwen Cochran Hadden's advice to heart, I discovered Letitia Byrd, a remarkable woman who had been involved with UMS for years. She had been attending UMS performances regularly and had been a member of the UMS Choral Union, our 180-voice volunteer choir that sang *Messiah* each December and performed at the May Festival. I made a point of getting to know Letitia, a widow who had recently retired from the Ann Arbor Public Schools, where she had been a counselor.

When I first visited Letitia at her home, I noticed and inquired about a collection of some 30 different-colored canvas tote bags underneath her dining room table. She told me that each bag represented a different community organization where she volunteered. There was a bag for the Ann Arbor Symphony, the First Methodist Church, The Links, Inc., Delta Sigma Theta Sorority, the United Negro College Fund, Packard Community Clinic, and many others. There was no tote bag for UMS. I immediately saw the opportunity in building a relationship with Letitia.

Around that same time, Ron Weiser and John Barfield, two leading businessmen in the community, were beginning to organize what would become an annual fund-raising dinner for the United Negro College Fund. The idea was to bring together people each year to celebrate and raise funds for a different historically black college or university. Having researched historically black colleges as a grad student, and seeking ways to become more involved in the community, I joined the executive committee of the group to help promote the event and sell tables to individuals and organizations.

At the beginning of one of the committee meetings, I asked if some members would stay after the meeting adjourned. I wanted them to know how grateful I was for the opportunity to work on the dinner and to get to know each of them in the process. I then said that as someone relatively new to the community, I wanted to know more about how the African American community felt about UMS. If the relationship needed to be improved, I told them, I would like to work hard to make that happen. Letitia, who also served on the committee, offered her help.

In the early fall of 1991, Letitia invited me and several UMS board and staff members to come to her home for a conversation with several prominent black members of the U-M School of Music faculty who were her friends. She had made it clear to me that she would be in charge of the meeting agenda. Among the first to speak was Ann Arbor native and U-M School of Music associate dean Willis Patterson. Describing his experience singing in the Ann Arbor Youth Chorus at the Ann Arbor May Festival in the early 1940s, he said how excited he was to be on the stage at Hill Auditorium with the Philadelphia Orchestra accompanying him. We from UMS smiled, appreciating that we had given young Willis this special opportunity. Then, using the exact same words, he described how saddened he was by the experience. We didn't understand. "I was sad," he said, seeing the confused looks on our faces, "because nobody in the audience looked like me." It was a punch in the gut. I hadn't realized that parts of our community could feel unwelcome at Hill Auditorium.

Then George Shirley spoke. He had recorded many "firsts"—first black man in the U.S. Army Chorus, first black music teacher in the Detroit public school system, first black tenor soloist at the Met. He was the Joseph E. Maddy Distinguished Professor of Voice at the music school and a new member of the UMS board. He delivered a message of hope, noting that he could see change on the horizon at UMS. He said he looked forward to working with us on making the changes necessary to open up the organization.

In addition to convening that meeting, Letitia assisted UMS in many ways. Importantly, she arranged for representatives of two organizations in which she was deeply involved, Delta Sigma Theta sorority and the service organization The Links, Inc., to help us diversify our audiences. We worked out an arrangement in which members of the two groups would join with the UMS Advisory Committee members to greet people at the doors of our venues, providing for some members of the community what Willis Patterson had lacked in the 1940s—welcoming faces the same color as their own. It was such a simple thing to do: to welcome people to your venue while sending the message that the assemblage was made up of people of all colors and cultures. The Links also purchased group tickets, bringing members of their community to concerts at Hill, many for the first time. Impressed by Letitia's long engagement with and commitment to UMS and her impact in helping us open up UMS, the UMS board nominating committee invited her to join the UMS board of directors. Her status as board member would become official in December 1993.

As we expanded our engagement with the African American community, we remained busy with many other projects in addition to the more routine work of planning events. One of these projects was renovating our office space. We saw it as an important part of our effort to modernize. And the way it came about was beautifully consistent with our goal of building stronger ties to the community and expanding its support of our work.

The idea of remodeling the office had its origins in 1989, when I was in the process of luring Catherine Arcure from Washtenaw Community College and hiring her as our development director. I spoke with Joe O'Neal, in his capacity as a member of the board of the Washtenaw Community College Foundation, about Catherine. He said the college would hate to see Catherine leave, but if she were going to leave, he wanted her to be successful and happy. For him, that meant working in a physical space of high quality. What he saw when he inspected our offices was pretty much what was there in 1936 when UMS moved into its Burton Tower offices: few private offices (and none in the development department), no air conditioning, and no carpeting. It was not a great environment for meeting with donors or cultivating prospects. Fortunately for us, Joe was a highly experienced contractor and the founder and head of O'Neal Construction.

In February 1991, Joe gathered together the leaders of the Ann Arbor construction industry and invited them to join him in updating the three floors of UMS offices. With their great respect for Joe, many contractors signed on to the project, which they committed to completing during the summer of 1991. The construction industry contributed $150,000 worth of design work, materials, and labor, and UMS raised the remaining $50,000 needed from individuals. U-M officials told me that they had never seen that kind of project done at the university. Joe's project added tremendously to the quality of our working space in the Tower, making a big difference for our work going forward.

Among the most notable of the events of the 1990–91 season was our presentation of the Metropolitan Opera Orchestra in April 1991. As recounted in chapter 3, I had received a heads-up about the Met's plans to tour in 1991 from the artist's management person handling Bernstein's 75th birthday concert back in 1988. He had told me on the afternoon of that historic concert that "the next big thing" would be the Metropolitan Opera Orchestra coming out of the pit and onto the stage, and I had signaled our readiness to participate in the tour. This early commitment allowed us to sign up to present the debut concert of the inaugural tour of the Met Orchestra at Hill Auditorium in Ann Arbor. To perform as the concert's soloist, we were able to book Jessye Norman, who received her master of music degree in voice at Michigan in 1968, had sung on the Hill stage as a student, had been presented professionally under UMS auspices five times beginning in 1973, and loved the Ann Arbor audiences.

The timing wasn't perfect. The concert was scheduled for April 30— one day before the Leipzig Gewandhaus Orchestra with Kurt Masur conducting would come for the four days of the May Festival. It was the only time the Met Orchestra had available for its brief tour, and we didn't want to pass on the opportunity to present them.

There was a point in the process leading up to the concert when we became a little anxious because we had not yet received a signed contract from the Met Orchestra. In the event the orchestra would be unable to perform in Ann Arbor, we needed a Plan B. Since UMS already had a separate signed contract with Jessye Norman for that date, we got in touch with her manager, Harold Shaw, and asked if Jessye would be willing to sing a solo recital in the event the Met Orchestra was unable to appear. Harold Shaw confirmed that she would indeed be willing to perform. Fortunately, everything fell into place a few days before the performance, and the Met Orchestra with Jessye as soloist gave us a spectacular and memorable evening. Jessye Norman performed both *The Death of Cleopatra* by Berlioz and "Brunnhilde's Immolation Scene" from Wagner's *Götter-*

U-M alumna Jessye Norman's sixth appearance on the UMS series was as soloist with the Metropolitan Opera Orchestra in its UMS debut on April 30, 1991.

dämerung, the fourth and final drama in the Ring Cycle. The orchestra would return in two years as the principal orchestra for the 100th Ann Arbor May Festival in 1993.

As we got further into the 1990s, UMS's transformation from a "go it alone" presenting organization into an organization based on teamwork was beginning to take shape. The collaborative spirit showed itself not only inside the organization but also in our relationships with other organizations and the community.

I had been pursuing a variety of ways of raising the profile of UMS in

Reception following the April 30, 1991 UMS presentation of the Ann Arbor debut of the Metropolitan Opera Orchestra. From left, Ken Fischer, U-M President James J. Duderstadt, Columbia Artists Management, Inc. Chairman Ronald Wilford, UMS Board President Norman Herbert, and Metropolitan Opera General Director Joseph Volpe.

the Ann Arbor community that went beyond traditional marketing and advertising. One effective partnership strategy was working with local radio stations. I would do on-air "pitching" for the University of Michigan public radio station, WUOM-FM, during its twice-a-year fundraising drives. In return, the station would publicize and sometimes even sponsor our events. This mutually beneficial relationship worked so well at WUOM that I was happy to replicate it when I was invited to do so by Eastern Michigan University's station WEMU, and eventually by WRCJ, the classical music station in Detroit. While I was on the air to encourage listeners to donate to the station, I was also able to talk about the partnership UMS had with the station. As premiums for listeners who would pledge support to the station, I would often donate tickets for our shows.

While we became more visible in the community, our intentions of stretching our aesthetic repertoire put us on the cusp of fairly revolutionary changes that would help us greatly expand who we could count as part of our community. In the fall of 1992, during one of our M-Team meetings, programming director Michael Kondziolka played us a recording of music by the Sufi devotional singer Nusrat Fateh Ali Khan. At a recent arts conference, Michael had learned of the artist's plan to organize a tour in the upcoming year, and he wanted us to consider bringing him to Rackham Auditorium. The music was so far outside our range of experience that we didn't know how to react. Michael told us that Ali Khan sang from the Koran and that in doing so he could transport people into a state of spiritual ecstasy. Michael said Ali Khan had a huge following and assured us the concert would sell out. We were intrigued and inclined to take the risk. Michael booked Nusrat Fateh Ali Khan for November 1993.

In the meantime, we continued presenting artists primarily within the Western musical canon. One performance that deserves mention because of its later significance was the Ann Arbor debut of the Italian mezzo soprano Cecilia Bartoli in the spring of 1993. Although opera was part of our standard fare, Bartoli's Italian identity allowed us to draw in members of the large local Italian American community.

About a year before her concert I was sitting in Bob Dascola's barber chair at the Dascola Barber Shop on East Liberty Street. Behind each of the eight chairs in the shop stood a barber of Italian ancestry, either a native or a descendant of one. Aware of the adage, "If you want to keep a secret, don't tell your hairdresser," I whispered in Bob's ear, "I'm bringing a wonderful Italian mezzo to Ann Arbor next season." Bob perked up. "Her name is Cecilia Bartoli," I told him. "Now, don't tell anyone until we make the public announcement." Bob stepped in front of the chair, crossed himself, and assured me that he wouldn't tell a soul. He told everyone, of course—exactly what I wanted him to do. By the time Cecilia arrived for her Ann Arbor debut, the Dascola barbers had been talking up her concert with such enthusiasm that the whole town was abuzz with anticipation and we'd sold out Hill Auditorium.

We took Cecilia into Hill for the first time shortly after her arrival. Accompanying her were her manager, Jack Mastroianni, a respected artist manager fluent in Italian, and his partner Brian Large, who was directing the television productions for the Metropolitan Opera. Cecilia took a quick look around the cavernous-looking space and gasped. "I can't sing here," she said. "It's too large."

I knew it wasn't her final word on the matter, but I wanted very much to make her feel comfortable. "Now Cecilia, it's going to be just fine—the acoustics here are wonderful," I said. "I'll show you." I told Brian and Jack to join me upstairs at the top of the balcony, as far away as you can get from the stage. Then I asked Jim Haven, the Hill Auditorium house technician, to bring out a bottle of seltzer water, one with fizz. We got everybody in place and quiet, and then Jim opened the bottle of seltzer water on the stage. Jack, Brian, and I heard the fizz clearly at the top of the balcony. With Jack giving a thumbs-up, I assured Cecilia, "You don't have anything to worry about, it's going to be just fine." And it was. The capacity crowd loved Cecilia and pianist Martin Katz. It was a huge success. After the show, Marguerite Oliver, an Ann Arborite of proud Italian roots and owner of Pastabilities, catered an Easter eve dinner atop the Rackham Building in the Assembly Hall. It was a spectacular spread. We began immediately to think about how we might get Cecilia back.

During the week of November 16–21, 1993, the Stratford Festival of Canada performed seven shows in Ann Arbor—four of Shakespeare's *A Midsummer Night's Dream* and three of Oscar Wilde's *The Importance of Being Earnest*. Colm Fiore and Lucy Peacock, two of Stratford's leading actors, were here for the entire week. It was UMS's very first foray into presenting theater, one that would initiate a significant expansion of the artistic genres within our presenting scope.

The Stratford Festival residency had its roots in the 1991–92 season, when Anne Charles, the Canadian consul general serving the four-state region that included Michigan, told me that I had to meet Colleen Blake, the producer of the Stratford Festival. Anne's intent was obvious. "You need to be bringing that company to Ann Arbor," she said, with considerable force. I said I was open to the idea and she arranged a meeting in Stratford, Ontario. Colleen and I met at Bentley's Bar, Inn & Restaurant and constructed a deal on the back of a napkin.

It remained for me to find a way to finance the affair. Having had success raising money from eight Ann Arbor families to pay the fee of the Pittsburgh Symphony when they came to Ann Arbor for the 1988 May Festival, we tried the same approach again for the Stratford Festival. When efforts to find people willing to contribute began to stall, some special friends in the community, including two from the UMS staff, stepped forward as guarantors to assure the achievement of the required funding level. In the end we accomplished our goal. The Ann Arbor Area Community Foundation gifted us $25,000, which not only provided a meaningful seal of approval for the project but also stimulated other gifts. That endorsement from our local community foundation meant the world to UMS. It was the largest gift that the foundation had made up to that time.

We originally did not have a Saturday matinee scheduled, but as tickets flew out the door and we could see a high demand, we decided we should schedule a Saturday matinee for November 20. Many in the UMS family thought it would be a bad idea as the Saturday matinee would go up directly against the always-sold-out Ohio State vs. Michigan home game. "Only an idiot would schedule anything in conflict with the greatest rivalry in sports," we heard repeatedly. But we as a staff were confident that there were plenty of people who would welcome an alternative to football that day, so we convinced the board and others that it would be successful—and it was!

Although the Stratford Festival residency was deemed a success by UMS financially and artistically, when we tried to get the Stratford Festival to return for the following year, they turned us down. We even sent a delegation of board and staff members to Stratford to try to convince them. We could never get a reason out of them for why they didn't accept. We think it might have been that they lost money, and as proud Canadians didn't want to admit it. Were that the case, we would have gladly paid them more.

We were eager to continue trying out theater so we looked elsewhere. Colleen Blake, the producer with whom we worked to organize the Stratford Festival residency, had left Stratford to take the administrative director role at Shaw Festival Theater, also in Ontario, and so we discussed possibilities with her. She and Shaw were delighted to work with us. Shaw brought seven shows to us during the week of November 15–20, 1994—three of Ben Hecht's *The Front Page*, and four of Shaw's *Arms and the Man.* Each was directed by Christopher Newton, Shaw's new artistic director.

More theater would follow. The Guthrie Theatre of Minneapolis would come for performances in January 1996, with two shows of *K: Impressions of "The Trial",* Garland Wright's adaptation of the Kafka novel, and one of Harold Pinter's *Old Times*, both directed by Joe Dowling. After that, we would take a break to study the three experiences we'd had with theater.

Immediately following the Stratford Festival residency was the long-anticipated Nusrat Fateh Ali Khan concert. It was our first real adventure into a culturally based professional presentation with significant commu-nity engagement.

We were incredibly fortunate to have Sardar Ansari from the local Indo-Pakistani community working with us to assure the success of the Ali Khan concert. Sardar not only helped us to build audiences but also to understand and navigate the cultural traditions of presenting an artist of Nusrat's stature. A few days before the concert, he called to make sure that we had 500 one-dollar bills ready. We were mystified. He told us that members of the audience would want to show respect by placing money at the artist's feet and might need change for their $20 and $50 bills. We made sure to have the one-dollar bills ready and planned to station a person in the lobby ready to hand them out as change as audience members arrived.

Then he let us know that no one from his community would be there at the concert's start time of 8 p.m. When we looked confused, he explained, "We just don't show up at the start time. This is a special event for us. We get dressed up and make an appearance." When it became apparent that we hadn't considered a special meal for Ali Khan and his ensemble, Sardar offered up a cousin with a catering shop who would bless and prop-erly prepare a meal. Without Sardar's gentle guidance, we would not have been as prepared as we were for what turned out to be a fabulous event. We realized that we still had a lot to learn about presenting performers beyond the limits of our cultural familiarity.

We also had a lot to learn about dance. UMS had been presenting dance for some time, but it wasn't what I would call "curated" dance. We didn't have a point of view. We were more or less responding to what was being offered us by artist managers as opposed to making thoughtful deci-sions based on our knowledge and experience with dance companies. This began to change around this time, thanks in particular to Andrea Sny-der and Peter Sparling. Andrea Snyder, as deputy director of dance at the National Endowment for the Arts, was always open to meeting me when I'd visit the NEA offices in Washington, D.C., and seemed to take a special interest in helping presenters like me who were seeking to educate them-selves about dance. Peter Sparling was chair of U-M's dance department and a former principal dancer with Martha Graham and José Limón.

My education in dance took a huge step in the fall of 1992, when Peter Sparling proposed to take Michael Kondziolka and me to New York City for a week to help us think differently about our dance programming. He arranged for the three of us to spend a day each with the dance companies

As UMS programming began to expand in the early 1990s, Ken and programming director Michael Kondziolka were immeasurably grateful to the guidance
from U-M dance department chair and former Martha Graham principal dancer Peter Sparling (right).

of Alvin Ailey, Merce Cunningham, Tricia Brown, and Martha Graham.
Peter was determined to educate us, and we were fortunate that he understood what we needed to become better curators of dance.

The big "aha" coming out of this New York dance tour was the realization that Martha Graham's centenary would be coming up in 1994 and that
the 50th anniversary of her seminal work *Appalachian Spring* would also
occur in that same year. Even though Graham herself had died four years
before at age 96, we could still celebrate her legacy. We realized that bringing the Martha Graham Dance Company to Ann Arbor could be the focus
of a new Lila Wallace–Reader's Digest Fund Arts Partners grant proposal.

Since the decision not to move forward with the Previn proposal, I had
done my homework with the board on collaborating with local groups.
We had seen the success of the Michigan MozartFest and the launch of an
education program for fourth graders, providing evidence of the value of
working with others. John Kennard's excellent work as director of finance

had given board members greater confidence about our fiscal situation. The board gave the go-ahead to begin planning for a three-week Arts Partners program that would feature the Martha Graham Dance Company in Graham's centenary year.

The Department of Dance, School of Music, Museum of Art, Center for the Education of Women, and Institute for the Humanities all signed on as U-M-affiliated collaborators. The Michigan Chamber Players, Washtenaw Community College, Ann Arbor Public Schools, and the Ann Arbor Symphony Orchestra likewise agreed to be community partners. We also secured the Library of Congress as a principal partner. The world premiere of *Appalachian Spring* had occurred on October 30, 1944 at Coolidge Auditorium at the Library of Congress, but since the Library was slated to be closed for renovations in 1994, we asked if we might have the honor of presenting the 50th anniversary performance of *Appalachian Spring* in Ann Arbor. The Library agreed and opened their treasure trove of Martha Graham and Aaron Copland photos and correspondence for us to look through and research.

We scheduled the Martha Graham Dance Company's residency for three weeks in October 1994, calling it "In the American Grain: The Martha Graham Centenary Festival." To recognize and celebrate the remarkable collaboration of a dozen different organizations that it represented, Peter and I wrote a statement for the festival program:

> We talked about the extraordinary impact Martha Graham had had, not only on dance but on music, theater, visual arts, and the lives of women. What better place to celebrate these milestones and to explore these many facets of her fascinating life, than on a university campus with strong programs in dance, theater, and music, with an outstanding art museum and humanities institute, and with one of the country's pioneering centers for the education of women?

Peter, as the festival's artistic director, worked closely with Graham artistic director Ronald Protas and I with managing director Barbara Groves. A month before the festival the Graham company invited Peter to reprise the role of Revivalist, which he had often performed with the company, for the 50th anniversary performance.

The festival began on October 23 at Rackham Auditorium with a concert of music commissioned by Martha Graham and performed by the

Michigan Chamber Players under conductor Stanley Sussman. They performed works by Gian Carlo Menotti, Zoltán Kodály, and Aaron Copland. Then there were four dance performances at the Power Center. Friday night's featured *Satyric Festival Song, Lamentation, Panorama* excerpts, *Cave of the Heart*, and *Acts of Light*. The Saturday afternoon performance was a family performance featuring *Appalachian Spring* excerpts, *Satyric Festival Song, Tjanang Sari*, and *Maple Leaf Rag*. Saturday night repeated *Panorama* excerpts and *Maple Leaf Rag* and added *El Penitente* and *Dark Meadow*. Thirty-three U-M dancers had the thrill of performing in the *Panorama* excerpts.

The fourth and final concert was the 50th anniversary commemoration of the premiere of *Appalachian Spring* that had taken place 50 years previously to the day at the Library of Congress. The first half, emceed by actress Claire Bloom, began with Copland's *Fanfare for the Common Man* performed by the U-M Symphony Band Brass under H. Robert Reynolds. Next the U-M Chamber Choir under Theodore Morrison performed Copland's "Long Time Ago." The Chamber Choir returned to sing Copland's "Promise of Living" from *The Tender Land*. There was a presentation on *The Making of Appalachian Spring: A Visual Retrospective* featuring materials from collections of the Library of Congress. The first half closed with reflections from the original cast members Pearl Lang and Erick Hawkins. Hawkins was ill and unable to make the trip to Ann Arbor, but he made a tape recording of his comments that we played while images of him from the original production were shown on the screen above the stage.

After intermission, a full performance of *Appalachian Spring* took place with live music provided by the Ann Arbor Symphony Orchestra and with Peter Sparling performing the role of the Revivalist with members of the company.

For several weeks before, during, and after the festival the U-M Museum of Art displayed original sets from Graham's ballets featuring artists whom she had commissioned, like Isamu Noguchi and Alexander Calder. With all these components, festival attendees had the opportunity to experience some of the rich musical and visual art that Graham stimulated through her association with a range of composers and artists.

Shortly after the Martha Graham Centennial Festival, on an otherwise unremarkable Wednesday, I attended, as usual, the weekly luncheon meeting of the Ann Arbor Rotary Club at the Michigan Union. It was my habit to head back to my office at Burton Tower at the close of this meeting, but on this day I decided to try something new. Being a member of the Rotary Club was a way of building relationships in the community, so why not follow up the luncheon meeting with some relationship-building in the university? Nearby was the Fleming Administration Building, which housed the offices of the university's executive officers, including those of the president and provost and the vice presidents for finance, development, university relations, student affairs, legal affairs, and so forth. Committed to the Peters and Waterman principle of "management by walking around," I decided to do just that. Starting on the highest floor (the sixth), I worked my way down to the first, passing by the offices on each floor. At each office, I asked the support staff person if the occupant was available for an impromptu chat. Most, of course, were away or busy. But to my delight, I had meaningful, albeit brief, interactions with the vice president for university relations, Walt Harrison, and the executive vice president for finance, Farris Womack. Without making appointments, I was able to make real progress building relationships with people I surely needed to know. I decided to visit the Fleming Administration Building twice monthly, leaving entirely up to chance the encounters I would have with the university's executive officers. It worked remarkably well. As long as I did every "Fleming Walk" with no expectations about who I would actually see, I couldn't be disappointed. If a productive conversation materialized, so much the better.

Always looming in the background, from my very first day as president of UMS, was the question of what should be done about the Ann Arbor May Festival. It was losing about $100,000 each year, and that annual loss was hurting the morale of the organization, not to mention our budget. But we couldn't just abandon it. The May Festival was a beloved institution in Ann Arbor, and many people were horrified that we were even thinking about changing it.

We had committed to seeing through the 100th May Festival in 1993; indeed, because it was the centenary event, we had devoted considerable effort to making it special. The Met Opera Orchestra had returned for its second time, with James Levine conducting, and it performed with soloists who had distinguished histories with UMS, including Itzhak Perlman and Renée Fleming. On the final concert of the Festival, the Detroit Symphony Orchestra and the UMS Choral Union performed Verdi's *Requiem*, a work that had been performed at the first and the 50th May Festivals. We

Banquet held at the Michigan League for the 100th May Festival.

also published a book that included highlights from each of the 10 decades of the festival, a complete listing of artists and repertoire performed over the 100 years, photographs, and copies of letters from artists and professional colleagues from around the world offering congratulations and sharing their memories of past May Festivals.

After this gala event, however, we had begun giving serious consideration to ending the May Festival and replacing it with something else. After the 101st iteration of the festival in 1994, we began a more formal process that included an analysis of the festival's strengths and weaknesses, as well as the opportunities it offered and the threats that it posed. (We borrowed this from a popular organizational development technique known as SWOT, or Strengths, Weaknesses, Opportunities, Threats, analysis.) The strengths and opportunities were its history, its celebratory nature, the special dinner associated with it, the outstanding orchestra, and the world-class soloists. The weaknesses and threats were its financial losses, the fact that it occurred when most students were away from campus, increased competition, declining audiences, and its length. Longtime subscribers were voting with their feet that a four-day commitment was more than many wanted. We agreed that what we needed to do was keep the things people really liked, move the orchestra residencies within the academic year so that students and faculty could benefit from them, and shorten the period of performances.

We kicked around ideas with the board and staff and came up with a plan. The event would be just as celebratory as the May Festival, but would last for just one day and include a gala dinner as an occasion for everyone to dress up. We would invite an established artist or ensemble with whom we had a long relationship to perform. Two key ideas were that the guest artist or ensemble would be awarded the UMS Distinguished Artist Award at some point during the event, and the performance would be a benefit concert for the relatively new UMS education program.

We went to Ford Motor Company to tell them about our idea for this new kind of one-day event. The Ford executives we talked with liked what they heard about using the occasion to celebrate a world-renowned artist and to raise funds for our education program. We invited Ford to become our major partner in the new venture. They would make a significant gift to support our education program and their top executives would serve as honorary chairs of the event, joining with the U-M president in presenting the UMS Distinguished Artist Award to the artist being honored. Ford committed $100,000, a gift of significant enough size for us to put their name on the event: it became known as the Ford Honors Program. What was critical to Ford was that their $100,000 not be seen as supporting a big gala concert and dinner but rather our education program.[1]

The 1995 May Festival was our final Ann Arbor May Festival, ending a 102-year tradition. Then we began planning the first Ford Honors event. Our first honoree would be Van Cliburn, who had last played for a UMS event in 1973, when he performed Rachmaninoff's Piano Concerto no. 2 with the Philadelphia Orchestra during the May Festival. The event was scheduled for May 11, 1996.

UMS commissioned Ann Arbor singer-songwriter Dave Barrett to produce a four-minute video on Cliburn's career that we would show at Ford Honors. Barrett set the video to the music of "One Shining Moment," the famous sports song that Barrett wrote that had accompanied the highlight film following CBS's coverage of the NCAA National Championship basketball game since 1987. The images were from a 1996 documentary on Van Cliburn directed by Peter Rosen.

In 1996, UMS presented pianist and Interlochen Trustee Van Cliburn with the
UMS Distinguished Artist Award at the first Ford Honors Program. With Ken
and Penny is Hill Auditorium House Manager Jim Haven, also an Interlochen
alumnus.

A couple weeks before the concert, ticket sales for the first Ford Honors Program were going very well, aiming toward a sellout of the 4,200
seats in Hill Auditorium. It was then that Cliburn's former partner, Thomas
Zaremba, who was living in Detroit at the time, sued Van for palimony.
This public dispute was an unfortunate distraction, but in our business
good news and bad news both sell tickets.

Zaremba happened to call the UMS ticket office to purchase a ticket
to the concert. Fortunately, longtime UMS staff member Sally Cushing
took the call and knew exactly how to handle the situation. She sold him
the ticket, made no mention of her recognizing his name, and did not tell
him where he would be sitting, only that it would be on the main floor.
Sally told me about the call. I wanted to give Zaremba a good seat but
also wanted to be able to keep an eye on him in case anything went awry.
We invited three people to upgrade their seats at no charge so that we
could have their seats on the main floor near an aisle and a side door. We
hired two large plainclothes public service officers to sit on either side of

Zaremba just in case he should try anything. Tommy was well behaved throughout the performance. Van Cliburn received a standing ovation at the end of his regular program. As the audience was sitting down for the encore, Zaremba remained standing, perhaps wanting to attract Van's attention. The stage lighting was such that Van wouldn't have seen Tommy in any case. He did sit down before the two public service officers had a chance to escort him out.

The event was a success from every perspective. We congratulated ourselves for having dreamed up a worthy successor to the venerable Ann Arbor May Festival. We were very happy, too, that instead of losing about $100,000 we ended up $100,000 ahead. The Ford Honors program would flourish for many years, honoring a diverse group of stellar artists.[2]

In the middle 1990s, UMS began to engage many of the communities of shared heritage in southeastern Michigan with whom we wanted to build meaningful partnerships. During this period, we formed relationships with leaders from the Arab community, the Mexican American community, and communities of people with Asian heritage. Most of these connections would have their most significant effects several years later. In the meantime, we built on the strong relationships we had already established with organizations and leaders in the African American community.

What would become one of our most important connections with the African American community had its origins in the fall of 1996, when a biracial violin major at the School of Music named Aaron Dworkin came to visit me at my Burton Tower office. Several faculty colleagues at the music school recommended that he meet with me about an idea he was exploring. Aaron told me he was tired of hearing orchestra leaders tell him, when he asked why there weren't more people of color in American orchestras, that such musicians "just aren't out there." Aaron saw it differently. "I know they're out there," he told me passionately. "They just need to be identified, encouraged, and rewarded." He was thinking about mounting a competition for young black and Latinx string players. His idea was to embark on a national search for talented string players of color, encourage them to send in audition tapes, invite those with the most promise to participate in a live competition, and then reward the best with cash prizes and performance opportunities. I liked what I heard from this creative and committed student and offered to help. I picked up the phone right there and made calls to several colleagues, letting them know about Aaron's idea. It wouldn't take long for it to become a reality and have impacts even greater than I expected.

One of the most important products of our efforts to work with African American musicians and artists was *The Harlem Nutcracker*, a work that UMS co-commissioned and then produced in 1996. The story of *The Harlem Nutcracker* began in the early 1990s, when I met the artist manager David Lieberman at a bar in the New York Hilton Hotel. David managed performers who had a point of view and were also deeply committed to community engagement, so I was very interested in what he had to say. When I told him about our efforts to build a stronger relationship with African American artists and audiences, he told me about the vision of choreographer Donald Byrd—to create a new version of the *Nutcracker* ballet that would have universal appeal but speak particularly to African Americans. Byrd's idea was to take the Billy Strayhorn–Duke Ellington score of the *Nutcracker Suite*, add some more music by David Berger, and set the Nutcracker story in Harlem. I was intrigued.

By this time, UMS had successfully co-commissioned several new works, so approaching other organizations that might want to partner in the effort to make *The Harlem Nutcracker* a reality seemed the obvious way to go. In 1995, I spoke to the leaders of two organizations in Detroit: Oliver Ragsdale, president of the Arts League of Michigan, an organization supporting African American artists and building African American audiences in Detroit, and David DiChiera, general director of the Michigan Opera Theater, who I knew was looking for further ways to engage the African American community. I asked each leader if his organization would like to be a co-commissioner of *The Harlem Nutcracker* with UMS. Both said they didn't have the resources at that time to do it but were interested in Donald Byrd's concept. I understood and hoped that there might be opportunities to work together in the future.

In the end, UMS became one of 12 organizations, including five other university-affiliated presenters, that commissioned Donald Byrd to create *The Harlem Nutcracker*. It was something of a risk: we were making significant financial commitments without knowing what the work would ultimately look like and how it would be received. We needn't have worried: the world premiere, at Arizona State University's Gammage Auditorium, on November 16, 1996, was a great success. The reviews were favorable, and the house was nearly full. UMS presented its first Ann Arbor performance of the work a month later, on December 18, at the Power Center for the Performing Arts, with four more performances following over the next three days. Ticket sales reached 90 percent of capacity. A similar run of *Harlem Nutcracker* performances was repeated in December 1997.

The Ann Arbor performances of *The Harlem Nutcracker* provided an opportunity to put in place a new strategy for connecting with community organizations. The idea, originally from Patrick Hayes, was to use a UMS event as a way for a community nonprofit organization to raise funds. The organization we worked with for *The Harlem Nutcracker* performances was Ann Arbor's Packard Community Clinic. UMS made a group of tickets available to the clinic at a discounted price. The clinic then added a tax-deductible amount and sold the tickets directly to people on their mailing list and to others who they thought might wish to both see *The Harlem Nutcracker* and make a donation to the clinic at the same time. The clinic netted $25,000 working with UMS. This was the first of many opportunities for local organizations to use UMS events as fundraisers rather than having to mount their own fundraising events, which can sometimes take staff and volunteers away from focusing on the fundamental work of the organization. Helping area nonprofit organizations raise funds also built a lot of goodwill for UMS.

The Harlem Nutcracker represented an important milestone for UMS because it incorporated many of the goals we had set for the organization: being more collaborative, taking greater risks, broadening our aesthetic scope, investing in new works, and presenting performers and works anchored in the perspectives of communities of color. It was one of the many achievements that made us confident about what we could do in the future.

Another confidence booster was financial in nature. At the end of June in 1996, on his last day in office, departing President James Duderstadt forgave the debt UMS owed the University. As a gesture of appreciation and an acknowledgment of the progress we had made, it meant a great deal to us. Even more important was its bottom-line effect. The debt had plagued us for years, overshadowing all our decisions. With the slate wiped clean, we felt liberated.

Notes

1. The grant from the Ford Motor Company enabled us to expand our educational and community engagement programs, which in turn resulted in us hiring Ben Johnson in 1996 as our first full-time education and audience development director.

2. The other artists to receive the UMS Distinguished Artist Award at the Ford Honors Program are Jessye Norman (1997), Garrick Ohlsson (1998), Canadian Brass (1999), Isaac Stern (2000), Marcel Marceau (2001), Marilyn Horne (2002), Christopher Parkening (2003), Sweet Honey in the Rock (2004), Guarneri String Quartet (2005), Dave Brubeck (2006), Mstislav Rostropovich (2007), Sir James Galway (2008), Royal Shakespeare Company, Michael Boyd, and Ralph Williams (2009), Michael Tilson Thomas and the San Francisco Symphony (2010), Renée Fleming (2011), Joshua Bell and Academy of St. Martin in the Fields (2012), Yo-Yo Ma and The Silk Road Project (2013), Wynton Marsalis and the Jazz at Lincoln Center Orchestra (2014), Valery Gergiev and the Mariinsky Orchestra (2015).

five
All Together Now . . .

On the 10th anniversary of my assumption of duties as president of the University Musical Society, my colleagues and I could confidently say that we had reached a good place. Although we were as committed as ever to what had made UMS distinctive throughout its history—presenting the finest in classical music—we had begun to diversify our programming and broaden our audiences, as we had set out to do. We were encouraging artists to spend more time with us, especially to benefit K-12 and university students. We had become more sophisticated and adventurous in our presentation of dance. We had dabbled in theater and learned a great deal. We had commissioned or co-commissioned 21 new works, consistent with our commitment to support creative artists. With our long-standing debt erased, we were on a secure financial footing.

Most significantly, though, we had successfully evolved the culture of the organization. We worked as a team, making decisions collaboratively, and we engaged with the surrounding community so seamlessly, as an integral part of the way we functioned, that we barely noticed the divide between the inside of the organization and the outside.

Nothing contributed more to our sense of accomplishment and pride in how far we had come in the previous decade than our response to a crisis earlier that spring. We were approaching one of UMS's most highly anticipated concerts, the completely sold-out performance of Cecilia Bartoli on March 29, 1997, when we faced one of a presenter's worst nightmares.

Cecilia had performed in Ann Arbor twice before and had developed quite a following in the community. She and I had also become good friends. The summer after her 1993 debut, I was in Vienna for a conference at the same time that she was going to be singing in Salzburg. I rented a car and went over to Salzburg, joined by Gillian Newson, who managed the King's Singers in Europe, and found a way to get in touch with Cecilia. She and I arranged to meet on Sunday morning at 9:00 a.m. at the train, where Cecilia would be saying good-bye to her departing mother. I met Cecilia's mother on the train. I had brought Cecilia photos of her Ann Arbor debut. With Cecilia's permission I gave them to mama, who loved them.

Cecilia and I enjoyed a coffee together, at which time I invited her to return to Ann Arbor for a second performance. She took in the invitation and said she'd let me know in the fall. I also learned that she'd be returning to Vienna the next day by train. I mentioned that I'd be driving back to Vienna with Gillian the next day, offered her a ride, and she accepted.

During the ride, I asked if she'd ever heard of the King's Singers. She hadn't. I played her a cassette of several of their songs and she was captivated by the countertenor voices. I asked her if she'd like to hear them live sometime. "Absolutely," she said. "How about tomorrow night?" I asked. "They're performing at Vienna's Musikverein. Gillian can get us tickets." That night we were guests of the King's Singers. At intermission, I went secretly backstage and told the guys that Cecilia Bartoli was in the house and suggested they "do something with that knowledge." One of their encores was Simon and Garfunkel's "Cecilia," which includes the line, "Cecilia, you're breakin' my heart."

Cecilia had returned to Ann Arbor on October 29, 1995 for a triumphant concert on a Friday evening before a Michigan home football game. We arranged for a tailgate in her honor at the Canham Natatorium near Michigan Stadium. The tailgate completely sold out. As I waited for Cecilia at the Bell Tower Hotel to drive her to the tailgate, I called Bob Dascola to tell him I would be bringing Cecilia by the shop so she could greet him, the other barbers, and the large Saturday crowd at the shop. I then called the *Ann Arbor News* and said that the biggest story in Ann Arbor was not the decision of the U-M president to resign earlier that week but was about to unfold at Dascola's Barber Shop. I suggested that they get a photographer there pronto. The above-the-fold color photo on the front page of the Sunday paper was of Cecilia with the barbers.

Since Cecilia was such a treasure, we had engaged her for the concert in the spring of 1997. It had the potential to become the highest grossing regular-season concert in the history of UMS up to that time. Her per-

UMS presented the young mezzo-soprano Cecilia Bartoli in April 1993, the first of four performances during Ken's tenure.

formance was set for a Saturday night at the end of March that happened (again!) to be Easter eve.

On the Wednesday before the concert, I got a call from Cecilia's manager, Jack Mastroianni. "I've got some bad news," he told me, "I'm afraid Cecilia's not going to have a voice on Saturday. She had to rehearse today in a hall in Akron where there was no heat and a significant draft of cold air. I'm just furious over it with the presenter. She'll sing tonight, but she's not likely to have a voice afterwards."

I hopped in my car, drove to Akron, Ohio, about three hours away, and found out where she was staying. I got there at 11:30 p.m. and sat in the lobby of her hotel. Her boyfriend at the time, Claudio, came into the lobby, saw me, and asked what I was doing there. I said, "I just want to know if Cecilia is okay; will you be seeing her?" He said, "Yes," and I assured him I was there to see her and support her.

The next day she woke up after noon. I invited her to join me for lunch at the hotel. She was distraught. In a whisper she said there was no way she would be able to perform on Saturday night. She felt terrible about it. I told her that I understood and that I supported her decision. I asked if I could take a message back to the people of Ann Arbor from her, and she nodded yes. As she dictated, I wrote down her words.

Driving back to Ann Arbor on Thursday afternoon, two days before the completely sold-out concert, I spoke on my very big mobile phone with our programming director, Michael Kondziolka. Most presenters, if faced with a cancellation of an artist of Cecilia's stature, would just cancel the concert, especially if it was just two days away. We at UMS, however, firmly believe that where there's crisis, there's opportunity. I had just spoken on the phone with my colleague Doug Wheeler of Washington Performing Arts. After I explained my predicament, Doug had suggested I consider as a replacement for Cecilia the talented and beautiful singer Denyce Graves, who had just played Carmen at the Met Opera in New York and was free on that date. I said to Michael, "I think we've got our substitute for Cecilia. We can get Denyce Graves."

Michael told me it was a good idea. "But I want you to consider someone else," he said. "Her name is Ewa Podleś—pronounced *Ava PODE-lesh*." I told him I'd never heard of her and asked why we should have her. "Because she deserves it," replied Michael. "She's got a magnificent four-octave range and needs to be heard. We're the people who should give her a chance."

I asked, "Where is she right now?" He said, "She was in New York this past weekend, where she gave a wonderful concert at Merkin Hall, but she's now back in Warsaw." I asked if she could be in Ann Arbor on time. "Yes, she'll turn right around and fly back with her husband, pianist Jerzy Marchwinski. Ania Marchwinska will be her accompanist." I asked if there was a review of the Merkin Hall concert. Michael said yes, and it was a great one, but it was embargoed for several weeks from now. I said, "How nice. We have a great review but can't use it." Having worked with Michael for 10 years and having come to trust his judgment about artistic matters, I completely supported his decision to go with Ewa. We got our marketing director Sara Billmann on the phone and decided to have an all-staff meeting first thing the next morning.

We mobilized the entire UMS staff, interns included. Doug Wheeler had suggested, when I had talked with him on the phone the day before, that we call every person who had purchased a ticket for Cecilia's concert. It would be a gargantuan task but we saw the wisdom in it. We printed out the list of purchasers, divided it into segments, and assigned 20 people the task of calling. We made sure they could all pronounce Ewa's name correctly. We began calling at 9:00 a.m. Friday. By Saturday at noon we had reached nearly every ticket purchaser, either talking with them directly or leaving a message: "We are so sorry to inform you that Cecilia Bartoli has had to cancel her performance; but we have a marvelous artist who will replace her. Her name is Ewa Podleś." I personally made the calls to the out-of-towners, many of whom were flying in for the concert. Many said they planned to come despite the replacement. To the others I made the offer of applying the cost of their tickets to a later event, but nearly all declined and didn't ask for a refund. They so appreciated the effort we made to reach them that they simply said that UMS could keep the money as a donation.

Then there was the matter of notifying the concert's corporate sponsor. It was Parke-Davis, the pharmaceutical company with a large operation in Ann Arbor. Its Ann Arbor leader was Ronnie Creswell, a native Scot who was often seen proudly wearing his kilt at special occasions around town. With Parke-Davis our most generous Ann Arbor-based corporate sponsor and Ronnie a member of our board of directors, I always gave Ronnie the opportunity to pick whatever concert the company would like to sponsor from among the season's set of offerings. At my suggestion, Ronnie had chosen in early 1996 to sponsor the Cecilia Bartoli concert. At the same time, he had done what he always did, which was ask us to reserve 100 seats and write a personal check for general support of UMS.

Once it was clear that Cecilia Bartoli would be unable to perform, Catherine Arcure and I tried reaching Ronnie right away. He was out of town and unavailable. We finally reached him at home late Thursday night with the news that Cecilia Bartoli had cancelled because she had no voice. I told him that we had engaged a replacement singer named Ewa Podleś but that he was free to withdraw the company's sponsorship, which included hosting a reception in the singer's honor after the concert, upstairs in the Rackham Building. "All your guests are expecting to see Cecilia Bartoli," I said. "Since that was part of the agreement, you have every right to pull out." Ronnie chuckled and made it clear that he would never abandon his commitment to support UMS. He said he would inform his guests of the special opportunity they would have to hear Ewa Podleś and affirmed his intent of hosting "as marvelous a postconcert reception in honor of Ewa just as we would have done for Cecilia."

There were 3,600 people in the hall that night, rather than the 4,200 who had purchased tickets to hear Cecilia. We had lost only 600 audience members. I stepped out on the stage to welcome them. "Ladies and gentlemen, thank you so much for coming," I said. "As you all know, Cecilia

Bartoli can't be with us tonight, but she asked me to deliver a message to you: 'To my dear, dear friends of Ann Arbor, I am so sorry that I can't be with you tonight, but a draft in the hall in Ohio was relentless and I lost my voice.'" I gave a subtle emphasis to the words "in Ohio." I looked up at the audience and saw nothing but smiles and understanding. When I welcomed Ewa to the stage, the audience stood and erupted in loud applause. This was before she sang a note. The audience understood that this relatively unknown artist was stepping in at the last minute for *the* Cecilia Bartoli and they wanted to let Ewa know that she had their full support and appreciation. I was deeply touched but not surprised by our audience's warm welcome to Ewa.

Ewa sang beautifully and movingly. The audience appreciated her every bit as much as they would have Cecilia. At the box office, we actually netted more in cash than we would have had Cecilia not had to cancel because the difference between her fee and Ewa's was greater than the amount we had to refund.

After the concert, as the several hundred guests gathered in the Assembly Room on the fourth floor of the Rackham Building, I brought Ronnie and Ewa to the front of room for a brief welcome and thank-you remarks. After I thanked Ronnie and Parke-Davis for their sponsorship, Ronnie asked for the microphone. In his Scottish brogue, he said that as a child growing up in Scotland, he would often listen to a recording that his parents owned of the great English contralto Kathleen Ferrier because he loved her voice so much. "I would say to myself that I will never hear another voice like it," he said, looking out at the audience. Then, looking straight at Ewa, he said, "Till tonight."

The next day, the specially crafted Easter brunch that Marguerite Oliver had planned at her home with Cecilia in mind went forward with Ewa Podleś as the guest. With only a few exceptions everyone who had signed up and paid for the brunch with Cecilia showed up to honor Ewa.

Later Cecilia communicated that she felt so badly about missing the concert that she wanted to come again as soon as possible. We were able to fit her in as the opener of our 1997–98 season on September 29, 1997, just six months after her cancellation. Another positive from the whole experience was that Ewa's Ann Arbor concert helped reinvigorate her career in the United States, where she had been largely absent since her Met debut in 1984. She told us afterward how grateful she was for the opportunity to sing in Ann Arbor. She would perform for us many times after that.

During the three short days between learning of Cecilia's lost voice and the postconcert reception, UMS staff members and I experienced a range of emotions ranging from the most chest-clenching dread and manic anxiety to uplifting joy and triumph. The whole affair was surely one of our finest hours. Seeing the exceptional level of teamwork displayed by every member of the staff as they dialed number after number, informing our audience of the change in artists, was something that would stick with me, vividly, forever. And on top of that were the standing ovations Ewa Podleś received both before and after the concert. I'd never been prouder of our organization and our audience. UMS had attained a new level of respect through our ability to come together and work as a team in the most pressurized of circumstances, while serving the needs of both our artists and the surrounding community that made up its audiences.

The ideal that motivated us at UMS more than any other was that, through music and the arts, we could bring people together. It was in the service of this ideal that we undertook a project resulting in a series of concerts that occurred just before the Ewa Podleś concert.

The University had done some research that indicated that while people in southeast Michigan were proud of the University, folks in the rest of the state thought U-M was remote and elitist. While that was an overgeneralization, of course, it bothered the people in the Office of External Relations. It was at that same time that UMS was exploring the prospect of mounting a special production that would enable UMS to work in partnership with colleagues in Grand Rapids, the largest city in western Michigan. We wanted it to be something big that we hadn't done before and could only do in collaboration with others. Walter Harrison, U-M vice president for external relations and a UMS board member, indicated that he was open to investing in a significant project that would bring Michiganders in the east and west together and might help alter the perceptions of those in the west.

The stars were therefore aligned. Given everyone's goals, we knew what piece of music we wanted as the focal point of the project: Mahler's Symphony no. 8. Often called the Symphony of a Thousand, it requires massive musical forces, both vocal and instrumental. When Mahler composed it in 1906, it was the first truly choral symphony because it incorporated

Over 400 performers from Grand Rapids and Ann Arbor perform Mahler's
Symphony No. 8 at Hill Auditorium in "Hands Across the State." March 23, 1997.

vocal components throughout. In addition to being the kind of work that
required collaboration, its themes were perfect for a project intended to
change how different groups of people thought about each other: Mahler
wanted the work to convey faith in the human spirit and the redemptive
power of love.

We recruited the Grand Rapids Symphony, the Grand Rapids Symphony Chorus, and the Grand Rapids Choir of Men and Boys from the
Grand Rapids area. The UMS Choral Union and the Boychoir of Ann
Arbor were the Ann Arbor partners. The eight vocal soloists all had connections to the state of Michigan. Altogether it involved more than 400
musicians. We called it Hands Across the State.

There were two performances at Devos Hall in Grand Rapids on March
21 and 22 and one in Ann Arbor at Hill Auditorium, on March 23, 1997.
All three were conducted by Catherine Comet. It was the first time the
Mahler 8th had been performed under UMS auspices in its entire history.

A message in the program book from former president Gerald R. Ford,
who grew up in Grand Rapids and went to college at U-M, set the stage

for these historic performances. Calling the project "a magnificent artistic enterprise" and a "unique collaboration," Ford noted that "the arts represent the very best in each of us. In music we express our creativity and our humanity."

We couldn't have agreed more. Our collaboration accomplished the objective Walt Harrison had in mind when he awarded the grant to UMS for the project. We brought together people in two quite different parts of the state in an uplifting project that could only be accomplished through collaboration. "We succeeded," Walt told us, "beyond my wildest dreams."

In the fall of 1996, the *Ann Arbor News* had announced that it would honor an Ann Arbor "Citizen of the Year" beginning in 1997. Along with several others, former Ann Arbor Public Schools superintendent Scott Westerman and I sent letters to the *News* nominating Letitia Byrd. We were very pleased when the announcement came out several months later: Letitia was being named Ann Arbor's first Citizen of the Year. Fifty-six others had been nominated, but the selection committee believed Letitia deserved the honor more than anyone. The headline of the front-page story was "Citizen of the Year: Helping Is Her Life." It featured a quote from Letitia that fit the theme well: "I like being part of organizations that do things, that make a difference in people's lives." The article listed 35 groups that had benefited from Letitia Byrd's generosity of spirit and time. UMS was one of them.

On December 7 of that year, as a way of thanking Letitia for all she'd done for UMS and for me personally, I took her as my guest to the 20th Kennedy Center Honors in Washington. Tickets to the event were prized possessions, but I had received two from former UMS board vice chair Marina Whitman, a top executive at General Motors, the TV sponsor of the event, who knew how much I had always wanted to see the Kennedy Center Honors.

Letitia and I flew to Washington on the morning of the event. Patrick Hayes, who played a key role not only in desegregating the theaters of Washington but in opening up the Cosmos Club to women members, insisted that we stay at the Cosmos Club. Letitia looked great as she came down the stairs of the club in a stunning black dress. Our ticket enabled us to attend the CBS reception in the Atrium before the event, and Letitia was thrilled to see Morley Safer and Walter Cronkite.

When we took our seats on the main floor, we found ourselves sitting

One of the most influential people in Ken's efforts to diversify UMS was Letitia Byrd (right), an African American community leader who was named Ann
Arbor's first Citizen of the Year in 1997. Also pictured is Bernice Johnson Reagon, founder of Sweet Honey in the Rock, a favorite of Ann Arbor audiences.

between former Michigan governor James Blanchard and Secretary of
the Army Togo West. Robert Guillaume and Sidney Poitier were sitting
in front of us and two Marriott family members of the Marriott hotel
chain were behind us. During the first intermission we chatted in the
lobby with Secretary of Education Richard Riley and during the second
intermission with attorney Lloyd Cutler of Cutler Pickering. The subject
of our conversation with each was U-M's affirmative action case, which
was beginning to garner public attention. Both men would support U-M
in its case.

When the program honoring Lauren Bacall, Bob Dylan, Charlton Hes-
ton, Jessye Norman, and Edward Villella was over, we headed to our table
in the Kennedy Center lobby for dinner. Letitia, who had met Jessye when
UMS honored her with our Distinguished Artist Award the previous May,
wanted to congratulate her in person. When we went to her table, Letitia
discovered that one of Jessye's guests was Vernon Jordan, President Clin-
ton's buddy and an old friend whom she had not seen in years. They had
worked together on civil rights issues in Washington in the 1960s. It was

Violinist Isaac Stern and Sphinx Organization founder Aaron Dworkin at the first Sphinx Competition. Hill Auditorium, February 1998.

a wonderful surprise for Letitia and a reminder for me of just how special and connected this woman was.

A couple of months after the Kennedy Center Honors concert, in February 1998, I was pleased to participate in bringing to life the music competition for black and Latinx string players that Aaron Dworkin had outlined for me in 1996. Aaron had since founded the Sphinx Organization as the sponsoring entity and was now organizing the very first Sphinx competition. He had raised cash and in-kind contributions well in excess of $100,000; these included a $10,000 gift from James Wolfensohn, president of the World Bank and chair of the board of trustees of both the Kennedy Center and Carnegie Hall. A gift from the Ann Arbor Area Community Foundation enabled Aaron to hire the Ann Arbor Symphony. Thanks to support from Dean Paul Boylan of the School of Music, President Lee Bollinger, and Senior Vice Provost for Academic Affairs Lester Monts, the University of Michigan provided the venue for the competition, which included Hill Auditorium, rehearsal facilities, and practice rooms.

As a former meeting planner, I was pleased to review with Aaron the checklist of tasks he had drawn up so that the competition would go without a hitch. There were 12 semifinalists from throughout the country. Making a special appearance at the competition was violinist Isaac Stern, who happened to be visiting in Detroit at the time. He was so impressed with the young competitors that he offered to give the winners lessons in his Manhattan studio.

One item Aaron had overlooked in his planning was hiring a photographer to capture images of the first competition. It was too late to enlist a professional, so I told him I'd be happy to be his photographer and would use a new Nikon that I had just purchased. Among the photos I took was one of Isaac and Aaron, which was later to appear in *People* magazine when Aaron was named a *People* magazine Hero.

In the spring of 1998, I received two phone calls that were to open up a whole new world of presenting at UMS. The first call came from University of Michigan Regent and UMS board member Philip Power, who, along with his parents, Eugene and Sayde, had funded much of the Power Center for the Performing Arts, which opened in 1971. Phil, a newspaper publisher and alumnus of both U-M and Oxford University, loved theater. He had just had lunch in the residence of the British ambassador to the United States, Christopher Meyer, and was calling to tell me that he had learned from Ambassador Meyer that the Royal Shakespeare Company was seeking to broaden its connections in the United States. The ambassador had asked directly if the University of Michigan might be interested in bringing the RSC to Ann Arbor to perform. Phil wanted UMS to consider this prospect and told me that he had made the same suggestion to U-M president Lee Bollinger.

The second call, from Barbara Groves, came shortly after Phil's. Barbara was the former managing director of the Martha Graham Dance Company and had been instrumental in helping UMS set up our successful Martha Graham Centenary Festival in 1994. Barbara was calling in her new capacity as advisor to the Royal Shakespeare Company. Her message was more of a command. "Ken, get to Washington right now. I want you to see the Royal Shakespeare Company performing *Cymbeline* at the Kennedy Center. The next day you will meet with Adrian Noble, the artistic director of the company, and I'm confident good things will happen as a result."

I did as instructed, saw the play, and met with Noble. He told me that the RSC was looking to mount the three *Henry VI* plays and *Richard III*, to be done in sequence as a tetralogy that would mark the new millennium. The plays—four of Shakespeare's eight history plays—were rarely done as four together, and since they were among Shakespeare's earliest plays, many dismissed them as "apprentice work." Adrian said that RSC was having difficulty finding British investors or sponsors who were willing to mount the four plays in England. He scoffed at the idea that the plays were amateurish compared to Shakespeare's other plays and emphasized their educational value. He said that the RSC saw great possibilities in mining the educational components of the history plays. I was enthralled by the idea of UMS offering a significant amount of educational programming to accompany the performance of the plays.

That conversation was the beginning of our courtship. Many conversations took place between UMS and RSC from 1998 to the end of 1999, during which we became increasingly interested. We explored the prospect of three annual residencies in sequence, beginning in 2001. The educational components would be emphasized, giving us a chance to engage many U-M academic departments in the venture. We were thrilled by the prospect, but could not anticipate how profoundly the Royal Shakespeare Company's planned visits would reshape our work.

A couple of other happenings in 1998 deserve mention. Zarin Mehta at the Ravinia Festival and Frederick Noonan at Lincoln Center invited UMS and six other presenters to join in forming Music Accord, an informal consortium where each presenter deposits an annual fee into a "bank" from which the group co-commissions new works, pairing composers with particular chamber music ensembles, solo instrumentalists, or singers.[1] It was a giant step in our commitment to invest in composition, something that in retrospect could be seen as existing in embryonic form in our first co-commissioning agreements for Bolcom's Sonata for Cello and Piano in 1989.

The year 1998 was also the first year of presenting *The Harlem Nutcracker* in Detroit, which was what I had hoped might eventually happen with this important work. After our two years of success with *The Harlem Nutcracker* in Ann Arbor, I had gone back to the Michigan Opera Theater and Arts League of Michigan to see if they were in a better position to collaborate with us. Both organizations were interested, so we worked out a plan under which we would copresent two more years of *The Harlem Nutcracker*, this time at the Detroit Opera House, which was twice the size of Ann Arbor's Power Center. We worked hard to engage the Detroit community, hosting special meals and community gatherings and market-

"Attack of the Ghouls" scene from Donald Byrd's *The Harlem Nutcracker*.

ing to churches, beauty parlors, community centers, and other gathering places. We opened on November 27 to favorable reviews. For the 12 performances in 1998, we sold 20,000 tickets, 61 percent of capacity.

On October 8, 1999, six weeks before our second season of performances in Detroit, *Detroit Free Press* publisher Heath Meriwether wrote about our three-way collaboration:

> How these very different organizations came together to present *The Harlem Nutcracker* is a story that holds great promise not only for arts organizations but as a model for how groups—rich and poor, black and white, large and small, city and suburban—can unite for the enrichment of everyone in southeast Michigan. . . . As important as all the enhancements and audience building has been, all three leaders believe the deeper benefit is in what people have learned about each other and their communities.

Lila Wallace–Reader's Digest Fund program officer Holly Sidford summarized the success of *The Harlem Nutcracker* in a way that was particularly gratifying: "What's happened here sets the standard for the nation. We've been tremendously impressed by the quality of the thinking and the thoroughness in which the community was consulted about how the arts can play a different role in bringing Detroit together."

One of a presenter's most important responsibilities is to play host. If musicians and performers feel well taken care of, and their experience in your city feels special to them in some way, they are more likely to come back and recommend you to their peers. Hosting had become particularly important for UMS as we moved in the direction of having performers stay for longer periods of time and building in various kinds of interactions for them with community members, U-M students, and K-12 students. And since we were a relatively small town, essentially competing with venues in cities like New York and Chicago, we had to stand out in some way by offering musicians and ensembles more than just good audiences.

I liked to think that my UMS colleagues and I gave top priority to the hospitality we provided our artists. Ann Arbor had always had a good reputation as a particularly welcoming place for musicians, but after more than a decade of working on raising the bar, we'd made it an art form. That was confirmed for me by a message of gratitude I received from Peter Riegelbauer, a string bass player who was also president of the Berlin Philharmonic, shortly after their concert at the end of October 1999.

Except for one unusual circumstance, we treated the members of the Berlin Philharmonic like those of any other international ensemble— which is to say very well. For example, we composed a message welcoming the orchestra to Ann Arbor on behalf of UMS, U-M, and the community, translated it into German, and placed a copy on the bed of every orchestra member before they arrived.

The unusual circumstance was that Claudio Abbado, the Berlin Philharmonic conductor, was ill with cancer. I arranged for one of our interns, Steven Jarvi, to be Abbado's driver. Steve was a second-year music student at U-M and an aspiring conductor. He was instructed to drive Abbado around as needed but not to fawn all over him because he might want to be studying his score or just relaxing. We suggested that Steve have some good questions ready to ask the maestro if he seemed up for a conversation.

Just before the concert, Abbado told me that he would attend the reception at the president's home after the concert if I would accede to a few requests. "Under normal circumstances," he said, "I would go back to the hotel immediately to rest. But knowing how important it is to you that

Berlin Philharmonic conductor Claudio Abbado responding to questions from U-M conducting student and UMS intern Steven Jarvi at the U-M President's House. October 20, 1999.

I be at the president's home afterwards, I will go to the reception, but I ask that you do me a few favors." He went on to list the conditions: "When I arrive, have the speeches but make them short. Put a plate of food in my hand. Deliver me to the corner of a room where I can spend five minutes with my dear friend Shirley Verrett, whom I adore." He paused and added, "And then have that young man who's driving me around—remind me of his name?" I said "Steven Jarvi . . ." "Have Steven come take me back to the hotel."

All that happened; speeches were short, food was delivered, Shirley Verrett (an internationally renowned opera singer from the 1960s to the 1990s and now a U-M faculty member) visited him for five minutes and then Steven Jarvi came by. "Mr. Abbado, I'm here to take you back to the hotel," he announced. "But first I have a few questions I'd like to ask you about your conducting." Abbado could have said, "Fine, we'll talk about it on the way to the hotel." Instead he invited Steve to sit down. Before they got into the questions, Abbado asked, "Can I smoke a cigar in here?"

It was not only the home of the president of the University of Michigan, but as a part of campus it fell under a strict no-smoking-anywhere rule. Steve was quite aware of that, but rather than inform Abbado of the prohibition, he said, "Let me go ask the president." He went to the kitchen and found Lee Bollinger. "Mr. Bollinger, Claudio Abbado wants to smoke a cigar in your living room. What should I tell him?" Bollinger responded immediately. "Claudio Abbado? He can smoke anything he wants in my living room." Steve went back to the living room, Abbado lit up his cigar, and they continued their conversation.

The last people to leave the party were Claudio Abbado, Steven Jarvi, the nine members of the Berlin Philharmonic Orchestra committee (out of respect for their conductor), and me. When Abbado and Steven were leaving the president's home, Abbado had a few parting words: "Young man, those were great questions. Come study with me in Salzburg this summer." And that's indeed what Steve would do.[2]

Our kind and thoughtful treatment of Claudio Abbado was among the many reasons Peter Riegelbauer cited for wanting the Berlin Philharmonic to return to Ann Arbor in the future. In the email he sent, Peter noted that the members of the orchestra greatly appreciated the hospitality we had showed them. It was important to them as well that we did not try to set limits on what they could perform: "You let us play Schoenberg when many other cities prefer we find something easier on the ears." But in Peter's explanations of why they had affection for Ann Arbor, what stood out the most was that we could offer audiences full of young people. "We look out in the hall and we see students everywhere," he said. "We don't see that in other cities." The other cities on their tour he was comparing us with were Moscow, Bonn, Paris, London, New York, Washington, Chicago, and Boston.

It was profoundly gratifying to know that our ability to draw an orchestra of the caliber of the Berlin Philharmonic had a great deal to do with our efforts to involve students in our activities. Yes, Ann Arbor is a college town, but it was not a given that students would attend our performances—we had to work to make that happen. We offered students discounted tickets, invested much effort in engaging them, and made the most of opportunities to involve our performers with the School of Music, Theatre & Dance. I was tickled, too, that our excellent hospitality was made possible, in part, by our strong connections with the U-M student body: only a music student like Steven Jarvi was in a position to devote so much time and energy to taking care of an ailing conductor and to derive so much benefit in the process.

In his email, Peter proposed that 18 members of the orchestra return to Ann Arbor for two weeks to play chamber music—not just to perform, but *to play with our students.* Of all the cities the orchestra could visit, Ann Arbor was the one where the musicians would most "love to come back and hang out." It was a wonderful endorsement of our town and everything we were trying to do.

Unfortunately, the only time the 18 musicians Peter had in mind could come was two years later in March 2001, right in the middle of the performance run we were planning with the Royal Shakespeare Company. That wouldn't work. But a smaller group of musicians from the Berlin Philharmonic, the Scharoun Ensemble, would come to Ann Arbor some years later for several days.

As 1999 was coming to an end, we let the Royal Shakespeare Company know we would like to move forward with the project that we had been discussing. In early 2000, Michael Boyd, director of the History plays, came to Ann Arbor to meet with us and do the preliminary planning. He visited several theaters and determined that the Power Center would be the best theater for the tetralogy. We were able to secure it.

At the end of Michael Boyd's visit, I quickly set up a last-minute dinner at the Moveable Feast, reserving a private room upstairs. I invited some of our donors. I tried to reach Professor Ralph Williams all day to invite him to join us but couldn't reach him. Ralph taught Shakespeare, among other courses, at U-M and had been awarded the Golden Apple Award for his outstanding teaching in 1992. As I was driving to the restaurant from campus, I saw Ralph on the sidewalk. I pulled the car over, hopped out, and opened the front passenger door. "Ralph, I don't know what your plans are for the evening," I said, "but you're coming with me." He got in the car and off we went.

When we arrived, the guests were seated. I put Ralph between Michael Boyd and me. After I introduced Ralph to Michael, the two of them immediately got into a deep conversation. I could tell they were hitting it off. Others of us were chatting among ourselves. After quite a bit of time had gone by, English professor Bob Whitman, seated opposite Ralph, said, "Excuse me, Ralph . . ." as if to say that there were others at the table eager to talk with Michael Boyd too. As Ralph began speaking with Bob, Michael

Boyd got my attention. Pointing to Ralph's back, he whispered, "We've got to get him to England. We've got to get him to England." It was clear to me that Ralph and Michael had really connected—hinting of a relationship that would become the soul of the partnership between the Royal Shakespeare Company, UMS, and the University of Michigan.

We looked to March 2001 as the time frame for the first RSC residency. We discussed the finances: RSC's fee for the project would be $2 million. Some of the fee would go toward the development of the plays and the remainder to their presentation and other expenses. It was a very large chunk of money, and we would have to depend on resources outside our regular budget to afford it. The residency was more than a year away, but we had to make our commitment to it 12 months ahead. This meant that in the next two months, between January and March, we needed to have a plan for how we would pay for the RSC residency. Raising that kind of money in such a short time for a special project like this would be a major challenge. I thought of another approach—finding a guarantor, an individual or organization willing to guarantee the fee. That would buy us the time we would need to find donors.

I decided to go to President Lee Bollinger and ask if the university would be the guarantor. Bollinger had spoken previously about how universities have a responsibility to support artistic endeavors, so I had some hope of success. When I made my request, Bollinger said he would have to think about it. I realized that the chances of ultimately getting an affirmative would be increased if I could guide him to the realization that acting as guarantor would get the university involved in something very special. With much help from Barbara Groves, advisor to the RSC and organizer of the RSC America board, we organized a dinner in early February 2000 at the Lotos Club on East 66th Street in New York City. Barbara knew just who to invite and orchestrated the seating arrangement. At each corner of the rectangular table was a representative of a corporation doing business in England. Dana Mead, head of Tenneco, Dana's wife Nancy, and Dennis Weatherstone, chair of JP Morgan, were there. Fred Koch, who had just renovated and restored the Swan Theater in Stratford-upon-Avon, was on the opposite side of the table from Lee Bollinger. To Lee Bollinger's left was Sir Eric Anderson, former tutor to Tony Blair and Prince Charles and now provost of Eton College. To Lee's right was Poppy Anderson, Eric's wife, an expert on King Henry VI and a member of the RSC board. When you consider the plays we were going to produce in the first residency—

Henry VI Parts 1, 2, and 3, and *Richard III*—it was all set up masterfully. After dinner, Lee and I left the Lotos Club and grabbed a drink. He said, "I'm in."

Three months later, in May 2000, President Bollinger was to announce that U-M alumnus Arthur Miller, class of 1938, one of the greatest playwrights of the 20th century, had given permission for a new theater planned for construction on campus to bear his name.[3] Seeing an opportunity for synergy, Lee invited me to use the occasion to publicly announce the plans that had coalesced around the Royal Shakespeare Company residency. I announced that, in season 2000–2001, UMS would be presenting a new international theater festival featuring the RSC and other leading theater companies. In addition to the RSC performances and activities, UMS would present the Gate Theatre of Ireland in *Waiting for Godot* and *Krapp's Last Tape* and Harvard's American Repertory Theatre in *King Stag* and the *Edda: Viking Tales of Lust, Revenge, and Family.*

We looked toward the RSC residency with great excitement. It would be a wonderful opportunity for UMS to better connect with the great university that we were part of. Theatrical productions of the history-related works of one of the leading figures in English literature presented nearly unlimited opportunities for scholarly and educational engagement. In what kind of society did Shakespeare live? What was going on at the time? What was so important about Henry VI that Shakespeare would want to write three plays about him? What role did theater play in England at the time the plays were written? These sorts of questions were ones that scholars on campus had answers to and were excited to explore. In this way we could build connections with the history and literature departments and, of course, the theater department. And these were only the beginning: the residency would bring opportunities for involvement by the physics department (exploring acoustics), by sociologists and psychologists and political scientists, and by scholars in women's studies.

Even as we held discussions about bringing to Ann Arbor a theater company organized around what could be considered the very core of the European cultural tradition, we were taking important steps to lay the foundations for presenting performers completely outside of this tradition. Back in 1995, I had come to the realization that forging connections with Michigan's Arab community could bring important mutual benefits. Detroit has the largest concentration of Arabs outside of the Middle

East, and since UMS was eager to partner with new organizations and to become relevant to different communities in our region, it was only natural that we look to the Arab community, with its enormously rich and diverse set of cultural expressions.

That's when I met Ismael Ahmed, at the time the long-serving director of ACCESS, the Arab Community Center for Economic and Social Services. We began our relationship without explicit goals for what we might accomplish beyond just getting to know each other. We enjoyed food together. We came to each other's events. We enjoyed being together. By the end of 1998, our friendship had deepened to the point when it seemed right to ask the three questions that I had learned about from Colleen Jennings-Roggensack, a leader in the performing arts presenting field who is especially skilled at building relationships among diverse communities. These are questions that should be asked only after a relationship has evolved to the point of being honest, genuine, and based on mutual trust. What do you want? What do I want? And what do we want to do together?

What Ismael wanted was some coaching and technical assistance related to presenting. ACCESS produced various kinds of events, and Ismael knew that UMS could help the organization put on better, more professionally produced shows. I said that UMS would be happy to help with that. "So what do you want, Ken?," asked Ismael. "We need to learn about the Arab world," I answered. "Teach us." We talked about how that might happen and in the process became known as Ish and Fisch. Ismael offered to host an "Arab Immersion Day" for the members of our staff and board of directors. Ismael and his staff would put together a set of experiences introducing us to elements of Arab culture and history that would include exposure to Arabic music, poetry, and food; study of "the map" to learn what constitutes the Arab world; and discussion of the diversity of religions in the Arab world. I thought it was a great idea, and we agreed to begin planning it. The third question—what can we do together?—resulted in brainstorming about projects that neither UMS nor ACCESS could do alone. Consideration of our shared goals pointed in the direction of presenting internationally known Arab performers.

Two Arab Immersion Days occurred in 1998, one in the spring and one in the fall. Members of the UMS staff and board took a bus to ACCESS headquarters in Dearborn each time, and we spent the whole day gaining greater knowledge, understanding, and appreciation of the Arab world.

We had learned from the Nusrat Fateh Ali Khan concert in 1993 that presenting a performer from a cultural tradition unfamiliar to anyone on the staff involved unexpected challenges in everything from performer hospitality to scheduling and audience expectations. Though we would certainly need help from the folks at ACCESS to present an Arab performer in Ann Arbor, our days of immersion in Arab culture made us feel up to the challenge of moving outside our comfort zone.

Notes

1. Music Accord, which at present has 12 members, has commissioned 37 new works in chamber music, instrumental recital, and song genres with more in the hopper. The total number of UMS commissions or co-commissions in dance, theatre, and music since 1987 exceeds 60.

2. A few years later, I was reading a review in the *New York Times* about conductor Kurt Masur sharing the podium with the Seiji Ozawa Fellow at Tanglewood. Who was that Fellow? None other than our Steven Jarvi from West Michigan. He went on to hold conducting positions with the Kansas City and St. Louis Symphonies and now guest conducts orchestras throughout the United States.

3. It was Bollinger's idea to pursue a relationship with Miller and name the theater after him. Recently, Lee told me, "I was pursuing this relationship . . . because I felt public universities were failing to recapture their history and make it part of their own culture. Given that Miller had described his days as a student at Michigan as the moment when he realized he was a playwright that seemed to me to be worth embodying in an actual theater."

six
No Limits

While the turning of the millennium in 2001 symbolized the beginning of a new era for many, it was the real thing for UMS. Theater, dance, and non-Western music became such a core part of our work and identity during the first decade of the 2000s that the programming of a typical season during this period bore little resemblance to its counterpart 10 years before. It was an exciting and rewarding time, made possible by years of hard work, steady progress in reaching for our goals, and support from our expanded community of stakeholders.

A crucial component of that support was financial. To implement our many ideas, we required income well beyond what we had become accustomed to. What we really needed was new, multiyear, institutional or foundation funding. The first critical infusion of such support came from the university.

In March 2001, UMS board chair Beverley Geltner and I had a meeting with U-M president Lee Bollinger and provost Nancy Cantor. We were requesting funding to support the expansion of our programming across all areas of the performing arts, but particularly our education and commissioning programs. I had a sense that despite the high regard in which UMS was held by Bollinger and other top administrators, their notion of the role we played in the life and mission of the university was limited. They were not likely to provide funding unless they grasped the depth and breadth of the value that we offered. I had therefore prepared for the meeting by thinking a lot about the relationship of UMS to the mission of the university.

If the University of Michigan's mission has three "legs"—teaching, research, and service—which of these legs, I asked Lee and Nancy, do you see UMS connecting with and furthering? They were quick to respond that UMS served the service leg of the mission, by providing public engagement and connecting the institution and the community. I agreed. "However, I'd like to point out," I went on, "that we are in fact serving the other two legs of the mission as well."

I then unveiled a substantial amount of evidence demonstrating how we served the teaching component of the university's mission. We were interacting with students in a variety of ways and providing value to them in the form of internships, master classes, workshops, access to artists in the classroom, pre- and postperformance chats, and discounted tickets to our events. They listened and nodded. Then I asked them what they thought the research part of the mission entailed. They responded that research was extending the bounds of knowledge in science, humanities, medicine, and other disciplines. I pointed out that creative work had to be included in the same category because it similarly extended the bounds of human cultural experience. And then I described how UMS, in commissioning new work, was stimulating creativity by helping artists in dance, theater, and music create new works and providing the vehicle for their presentation. I noted that each time one of our commissions was performed at Suntori Hall in Japan, at the Barbican in London, and at the Châtelet in Paris, it bore the name of the University of Michigan, just as a physics monograph bore the name of its U-M faculty author. So, I said in summary, UMS is contributing to each leg of the university's mission—but what it does for the research and teaching components of the mission does not produce income. If UMS is going to continue to provide the university value in those areas, it needs financial support.

Lee asked how much support I needed. I said $750,000 a year. He countered, "All I've got is $500,000." I responded, "How about six and we have a deal?" He thought a moment and said, "Okay." Thanks to Lee Bollinger, UMS had an infusion of $600,000 for the 2001–02 season that we devoted to our education and commissioning programs.

Partway through the 2001–02 season, Lee Bollinger was named the 19th president of Columbia University. He would assume office on June 1, 2002. After the announcement of the Columbia appointment but before Lee left Michigan, I wrote up a document putting forth my argument concerning UMS's contributions to all three parts of the university's mission and proposed that it include language guaranteeing that U-M would support 9 percent of UMS's budget each year. Lee didn't disagree with my argument, but it was no surprise that he wasn't willing to commit his successors to the amount. In the document he urged his successors to meet annually with UMS representatives and hoped that "UM will seriously consider providing support for . . . education (teaching) . . . creation (research) . . . and presentation (service)."

The University's contribution would continue each year thereafter, with some ups and downs along the way depending on the fiscal situation at U-M. A delegation from UMS that always included the board chair and me would meet each year with the president and provost after the first of the calendar year to report on our current and future activities and request support for the coming season.

In early 2001, we devoted considerable energy to preparing for the upcoming Royal Shakespeare Company residency in March. On the creative side, an extraordinarily productive collaboration had already begun between Director Michael Boyd and U-M professor Ralph Williams. Michael and Ralph had really hit it off when they first met at the impromptu dinner I'd hosted the year before. Shortly thereafter, Michael had engaged Ralph as an advisor on the tetralogy project and invited him to England to begin working together. Of that invitation, Ralph later wrote:

> When I was approached after our first conversation, which ranged over Shakespeare's plays, about coming to England to participate with him [Boyd] and the cast in conceiving the productions, I felt it would be absurd not to engage. For I had already the sense of being at the beginning of what in fact our relationship has been for me, a seamless joining of the personal, the professional, and spiritual in a friendship which in part defines a life.

Ralph told me that his first visit to England established the contours of what followed. Michael and Ralph discussed the plays; Ralph sat in on auditions in London for casting; they discussed ways in which one might conceive most fruitfully this coming together of two great institutions in a joint project—one which, on the side of the University, would draw faculty and students into close contact with a creative project and its realization. At the end of that visit, Michael said to Ralph, "Now we need you at least twice more." In fact, Ralph went to England a total of five times in the preparatory year. Ralph would characteristically come to the rehearsal room, sit in on rehearsals, write notes for Michael to consider, and greet the cast. "I was able to give the cast in an arduous project a sense of the warm and eager support of the University community," wrote Ralph, "and carry back to the University reports on the progress of rehearsals for the plays." The insight Ralph had on what was developing informed the series of four well-attended lectures he gave in 1,100-seat Rackham Auditorium before the residency itself, and helped us prepare for the residency and performances.

The Royal Shakespeare Company arrived in Ann Arbor a week before the opening performances scheduled for Saturday, March 10. Everyone was excited about the company being in town. On Monday, March 5, we held "A Royal Welcome" at the Power Center—a chance for Ann Arborites to meet the company, preview the transformed theater with its thrust stage and onstage seating, and enjoy authentic ales, fine wine, and regal fare. President Bollinger and I welcomed the ensemble, and RSC director Michael Boyd gave us a preview of what we were in for. Those who attended the event learned that Michael had cast the black actor David Oyelowo in the title role of the English king Henry VI. He would be the first actor of African heritage to play an English king in a major Shakespeare production.[1]

The statement in the front of the program book described the upcoming 12 performances and 75 educational events as "the fruit of three years of planning [that] draw on the great range of skills and knowledge built up in the long history of our cultural institutions." It noted: "Our present effort grows from our belief that artists, scholars, and learning audiences of all ages can, in coming together, gain unparalleled access into the vast imaginative sweep and dramatic power of the greatest user of words in our language."

The performance schedule was dense and ambitious. On Saturday, March 10, there would be one performance each of *Henry VI, Part 1*; *Henry VI, Part 2*; *and Henry VI, Part 3*. *Richard III* would be performed the following day. Then all four plays would be performed again during a three-day stretch beginning on Tuesday. The initial sequence would then be repeated the next weekend, March 17 and 18.

Seeing the three *Henry VI* plays in one day at first seemed like it might be too much for people. Would audience members be OK sitting for three-plus hours for each of three plays, all in the same day, for a total of more than 10 hours? We needn't have worried. It turned out that people couldn't get enough of it. They picked up the box lunches we served between the first and second plays, devoured the contents wherever they could find a space, and hurried back into the theater so as not to miss anything.

The plays were riveting in their dialogue, pacing, and movement. Michael Boyd had the characters using every inch of the theater. They flew down ropes tied to the stage ceiling. They entered from the back of the house, and all of a sudden King Louis XI of France was standing in the aisle giving a speech. Richard Plantagenet, the Duke of York, appeared from under the floor through the vomitorium. To accommodate the high ticket demand and add to the sense of "theater in the round," about 200 people were able to sit on risers on the stage itself. While no audience member was injured during the sword fights, fake blood did find its way onto the clothing of a few patrons. Nearly 17,000 people, coming from 30 states and 5 countries, attended the 12 performances.

The performances were only part of the magic. Highlights among the 75 public and private educational events included interviews of Michael Boyd by Ralph Williams and RSC artistic director Adrian Noble by President Lee Bollinger. A four-part series titled "Staging History" was designed to share a unique behind-the-scenes look at how the RSC developed the tetralogy technically and artistically. Zingerman's Deli hosted "A Taste of the British Isles" where RSC members joined the community in sampling a variety of cheeses. At the Detroit Public Library's Main Downtown Library, several RSC actors hosted English high tea, giving the library a chance to dust off a historic English silver service that had not been used since the 1930s. RSC actors, crew, and staff visited numerous classes throughout the University. After the final performance, there was a RSC Goodbye Party, open to the public, at Leopold's Brewery & Greenhouse.

During the Royal Shakespeare Company's residency, two first-year students, Taryn Fixel and Megan Marod, were heavily involved in the activities. Before the company's arrival, they had made it known to me that the RSC's Ann Arbor visit was the greatest thing they could imagine happening and they wanted to help out and spend time with the actors. As I expected, they took full advantage of the company's presence, meeting actors and directors and attending all the postperformance activities. When the residency was over they came to Ralph Williams and me and asked if we could help get them a summer of experience working with the

RSC in England. Ralph and I suggested they write a proposal. In it they expressed their enthusiasm and said they would do any kind of work, even cashiering at the gift shop. We made some edits and sent it off to Michael Boyd. Michael wrote back, noting, "No Michigan student works in the gift shop; they become assistant directors." That meant so much to all of us. Ralph helped Taryn and Megan come up with some money to make it possible for them to go over to England for 12 weeks during the summer. They worked as assistant directors for the RSC and developed friendships that would impact their lives significantly.

The Royal Shakespeare Company residency overall exceeded our expectations for impact. We engaged many students and professors in many U-M departments, brought in people from the community who had never before attended one of our events, and established ourselves as presenters of top-flight theater. We were completely reassured that planning for two additional RSC residencies in the years to come was the right thing to do.[2]

In the spring of 2001, Ismael Ahmed and I got back together to follow up on our commitment to do a project together. Our discussions coalesced around Simon Shaheen, a Palestinian-born oud player who had trained as a violinist in the United States. Shaheen seemed a perfect choice for the role of ambassador of cross-cultural understanding. Though of Palestinian descent and Arab ethnicity, he was Catholic. He was a citizen of both Israel and the United States. He had experience exposing Americans to Arab music and culture. Ish and I wanted to bring him and his ensemble, Qantara, to Dearborn and Ann Arbor for an extended residency. We put together a proposal and submitted it to APAP in June, seeking a grant to support the extensive planning required for such a residency. We were waiting to hear the results of our proposal when nearly 3,000 people died in the terrorist attacks of September 11, 2001.

I was in New York City on 9/11. When I learned the perpetrators were Arab, I called Ish right away because I could imagine what he, ACCESS, and the Arab community might be facing. I asked him how he was doing and how we at UMS could help. He thanked me for the call and noted that he had received an earlier call from William Clay Ford Jr., chairman of the Ford Motor Company, offering his assistance. Ish had a good relationship with Ford Motor Company and knew many of its executives. Ish noted how much it meant to have a corporate leader of Ford's stature call and offer support.

The planning proposal that ACCESS and UMS had put together was reviewed in the late fall of 2001, and the committee was surprised to learn that we had been building a relationship for a long time, one that predated the September 11 attacks. This led to the full funding of our planning proposal and later to significant funding for the project itself. We looked forward to bringing Simon Shaheen to our region. He would be able to spread out his time with us over a two-month period bridging the end of 2003 and the beginning of 2004.

A little more than a year after the RSC residency, Lee Bollinger left Michigan to assume the presidency of Columbia University and Joe White, the dean of Michigan's business school, became interim president of U-M. I was worried that the change in leadership might endanger the university's support of the upcoming second RSC residency. Joe White, however, committed to providing a grant of $2 million that would enable UMS to continue our relationship with the Royal Shakespeare Company. This support was critical because Hill Auditorium was to be closed between May 2002 and January 2004 for restoration and renovation work, requiring us to rent much smaller venues, dramatically reducing our income potential.

Meanwhile, at his new perch at Columbia, Lee Bollinger expressed his desire to remain engaged with the Royal Shakespeare Company. This set the stage for a new collaboration. Lee and I developed a joint interest in making it possible for Salman Rushdie's novel *Midnight's Children* to become a stage play produced and performed by the RSC. This dense novel, about the partition of India in 1949, won the Booker Prize for Fiction in 1981 and then the special "Booker of Bookers" award in 1993; it was clearly a landmark work. Salman Rushdie had wanted to do a film or stage adaptation for a long time, but no other parties committed support until Lee and I stepped forward. With Bollinger committing funding from Columbia, and with the University of Michigan supporting UMS in the endeavor, we agreed to co-commission, with RSC, Rushdie's adaptation of the novel for the stage. The play would have its U.S. premiere during the second RSC residency in March 2003.

In the early fall of 2002, a press conference was scheduled to announce that Columbia and Michigan were going in together to invest in a stage adaptation of *Midnight's Children* that would be performed by the Royal Shakespeare Company. This was a big deal for the RSC and a big deal for Salman Rushdie, so the RSC arranged to hold the press conference at the

A scene from the Royal Shakepeare Company's stage adaptation of Salman Rushdie's Midnight's Children.

Bryant Park Hotel Auditorium, not far from Times Square in New York City. There would be four speakers: Susie Sainsbury, vice chair of the RSC board and part of the Sainsbury grocery store family, would speak first, followed by Salman Rushdie, Lee Bollinger, and me.

Susie Sainsbury expressed excitement about the project and appreciation to Columbia and UMS for supporting the project. Rushdie spoke eloquently about his award-winning work and thanked the RSC, Columbia, and UMS for making the commitment that allowed him to fulfill his dream of creating the stage adaptation. Then Lee made a beautiful case for why it was the responsibility of the great universities in the United States to support creative artists like Rushdie.

When it was finally my turn, I began by remarking how wonderful it was to be working with Lee again to do something special together as we had done the previous year when we helped produce and present the four history plays of Shakespeare at Michigan. I continued that I couldn't agree with him more that great universities had an important role in supporting the creative artists of our time and in presenting their work. Then I said that everyone in the room should know which university in the United States had supported more creative work in the last seven years than any other. After a pause, I identified that institution as the University of Iowa. Everyone looked a little incredulous. I explained that during the last seven years Hancher Auditorium at the University of Iowa, under the leadership of Wallace Chappell, had commissioned more new work in dance, theater, and music than any other university presenter in the United States, and that these were significant works for the Joffrey Ballet, the Kronos Quartet, and other major artists. "Two weeks ago," I continued, "the regents of the University of Michigan selected as our next president the woman who oversaw all of that creative activity as president of the University of Iowa; her name is Mary Sue Coleman and she's coming to the University of Michigan."

Despite tooting my own university's horn about its support of the arts and creative endeavors, however, what I really wanted was to have universities all over the country doing it as much and as well as possible. It was with that goal in mind that earlier that year I had joined three of my most cherished colleagues—consultant Jerry Yoshitomi, Mike Ross of University of Illinois–Urbana Champaign, and Colleen Jennings-Roggensack of Arizona State University—in founding the Major University Presenters (MUPs) network. We set up MUPs as an affinity group of performing arts presenters on major university campuses that could be instrumental in strengthening the programs of member organizations through idea sharing, co-commissioning, integrating arts and academics, and supporting foreign travel and research projects. Members would take turns hosting MUPs meetings on their respective campuses, giving each of us an opportunity to put forth our unique hospitality, show off our venues, and engage our universities' leadership. As it grew and matured, MUPs served all the functions we envisioned for it and more.

The year 2003 opened with Sweet Honey in the Rock, the Grammy Award–winning African American female a cappella ensemble, performing on January 10 at the Michigan Theater the world premiere of *An Eveningsong*, a piece commissioned by UMS and several other U.S. presenters commemorating the ensemble's 30th anniversary. Performing along with Sweet Honey that evening in early January was Big Lovely, a group led by Toshi Reagon, the daughter of Sweet Honey founder Bernice Johnson Reagon.

Sweet Honey in the Rock had performed in Ann Arbor four times before, beginning in 1993, and our community had grown extremely fond of the group and its music, which had deep roots in the sacred music of the black church—spirituals, hymns, gospel—with influences from jazz and blues. As part of this visit, Sweet Honey was doing a series of performances in the schools, organized by our Youth Education Program, that would involve about 2,800 students. Since Sweet Honey traveled with its own sign-language interpreter, among those students would be about 200 deaf children and their friends.

Sweet Honey in the Rock's visit was significant enough, but of even greater import may have been what came of it. Attending the performance was UMS board member Marvin Krislov, who, as the university's general counsel, was a key leader in defending the university's affirmative-action admissions policies, which were being tested in two cases soon to come before the Supreme Court. Moved by the performance and its messages of justice, Marvin had an idea.

About a month before U-M would be arguing the cases before the Supreme Court, scheduled for April 1, 2003, I got a call from Marvin. He was thinking ahead about the rally in Washington that U-M would hold on the eve of the Supreme Court hearing. He was imagining there would be a series of speeches but believed that speeches wouldn't be enough to inspire those arguing the cases the next day. He had a vision of Sweet Honey in the Rock singing the great freedom songs of the civil rights movement and of their inviting the rally group to join in on some of them. Marvin knew that what we needed to go up to Capitol Hill with our hearts and minds filled with the rightness of our position was the music of Sweet Honey. Marvin asked if I'd call Bernice Johnson Reagon and see if Sweet Honey in the Rock would be willing to participate.

Bernice liked the idea. After consulting with her Sweet Honey sisters, she called back to say that they'd be honored to participate and would gladly contribute their services, recognizing the importance of the cases. They came to the rally and, just as Marvin had envisioned, they closed the event by singing a few numbers alone and then had us all join in on some others. In a gesture of gratitude, Marvin and U-M president Mary Sue Coleman presented each member of Sweet Honey with signed copies of the two briefs that had been filed with the Supreme Court. Then we waited a few months for the decisions. They were announced on June 23: Michigan prevailed in one of the cases, on the admissions policies of the law school, but narrowly lost the second. It was a mixed result that forced

U-M to alter the specifics of its policies but not to abandon the general principle of affirmative action.

A year later, on May 15, 2004, UMS presented Sweet Honey with our UMS Distinguished Artist Award at the ninth Ford Honors Program at Hill Auditorium. At that event, Bernice told me that singing at the Supreme Court rally was one of the most important and most inspiring moments in Sweet Honey's history as a group.

The biggest event of 2003 was the second Royal Shakespeare Company residency in March. It followed the same general formula as the highly successful first residency: a series of performances over a 16-day period accompanied by roundtable discussions, "Insights" presentations, artist interviews, workshops for students, faculty lectures, and other educational activities. This time only two Shakespeare plays were presented— *The Merry Wives of Windsor* and *Coriolanus*—but the program included six performances of the new dramatization of Salman Rushdie's *Midnight's Children*. The Rushdie play, given its U.S. premiere in Ann Arbor before it went on to the Apollo Theater in New York City, was the work UMS had co-commissioned with Columbia University. We were pleased to see the results of our investment and to have Mr. Rushdie participate in preperformance activities in Ann Arbor.[3]

Attendance figures for the performances of the first RSC residency had been impressive, but those for the second were even better: 19,786 people attended the 16 performances. And by our best estimates, a total of nearly 10,000 people participated in the more than 50 educational events in partnership with over 25 university, school district, and community organizations.

Simon Shaheen was in Ann Arbor for his long-awaited residency in January 2004. As part of the residency, Simon visited schools, led workshops on Arabic music for area musicians, sat for interviews, and took part in other educational sessions. Simon and his ensemble Qantara, whose artists represented many musical traditions and nationalities, ended the residency with a concert on January 31 at Ann Arbor's Michigan Theater. The concert featured the world premiere of a piece Simon composed that he titled *Arboresque*, in recognition of Ann Arbor. The work featured not only Qantara but several local musicians whom Simon had met during the residency, who played traditional Arabic instruments such as the qanun, nay, mizmar, and mijwiz. By the end of the concert, I had the feeling that through all the activities of the residency we had accomplished our goal of cultivating in our audiences an understanding and appreciation of Arab music and culture.

Later that winter, I met again with Ismael and Anan Ameri, the associate director of ACCESS. UMS was in the process of planning our first Arab World Music Festival, which would occur during the 2004–05 season. Leveraging what we had already accomplished with the Simon Shaheen residency, it would feature music from all over the Arab world. We were counting on ACCESS to help us with the planning. Ish and Anan told me, however, that they were going to have to redirect their attention during that season to the opening of the Arab American National Museum in Dearborn, the first of its kind in the United States. They were planning the opening for May 5, 2005 (at 5 p.m., no less!) and would need the full year to finish fundraising and other tasks.

I was devastated at the prospect of losing their invaluable help. "Don't worry," they said. "There are 7,000 Arabs in Ann Arbor. We're going to introduce you to four of them, all amazing women, and they will see that you receive the support from our community for the Arab World Music Festival." The women they identified were Wadad Abed, Huda Karaman Rosen, Rabia Shafie, and Liz Othman.

The four of them organized five dinners, each in the home of a leader in the Arab community. There was delicious Middle Eastern food. After dinner there was Arabic poetry and music. I was then invited to describe the festival in five minutes, but not to promote it. That, the women said, was their job. They encouraged everyone to attend and thanked UMS for focusing on and celebrating the art and culture of the Arab world. In the aftermath of 9/11, we all saw the festival as a counterpoint to the hostility that many in the Arab community were experiencing. I found Wadad, Huda, Rabia, and Liz to be friendly, well connected, and passionate about helping us be successful with our Arab programming.

We worked to set up a series of performances that would be distributed throughout the 2004–05 season. Lebanese composer and oud master Marcel Khalifé and the Al Mayadine Ensemble would kick it off on October 16, 20045. Ensemble Al-Kindi and the Whirling Dervishes of Damascus would follow a month later on November 14. Then we would have Sam Shalabi and the Osama Project in January 2005, and close out with Malouma on April 9 and Songs of the Sufi Brotherhood on April 10.

Ken, Ann Arbor businessman Tom McMullen, Mikhail Baryshnikov, and local restaurateur Dennis Serras after a golf game during Baryshnikov's performance residency in Rezo Gabriadze's *Forbidden Christmas* (October 2004).

As a natural connector and facilitator, one of the things I loved about my job was introducing people who I knew had shared interests and were likely to enjoy each other's company. With all the relationships I had established with both local donors and performers from around the world, there were many opportunities to connect people who might not otherwise have met each other. I saw one such opportunity in late October 2004, when Mikhail Baryshnikov was in town for more than a week for a six-performance run of Rezo Gabriadze's *Forbidden Christmas, or The Doctor and the Patient.*

When my UMS colleagues and I learned at the beginning of the week that Baryshnikov would enjoy playing golf during his weeklong residency, we arranged for the avid golfers on our staff—John Kennard, Patricia Hayes, and Joanne Navarre—to play with him at the Ann Arbor Country Club on his first day to see what kind of golfer he was. Joanne ended up not playing but rode along on the golf cart. Instead, her husband Gerry and club pro Frank McAuliffe made it a fivesome. Baryshnikov (who wanted us to call him Misha) demonstrated that he was a fine golfer; he shot an 88.

I then imagined that some of our corporate sponsors might enjoy playing with him on the other days. I invited local real estate developer Tom McMullen to play golf with Misha on the second day. Tom at first thought it was a joke. When he realized it was a sincere invitation, he accepted and when asked if he knew someone else who'd like to join the group, Tom suggested restaurateur and UMS sponsor Dennis Serras. I rounded out the foursome, and we played 18 holes on the U-M course. Misha knew he was in for fun when Dennis commented as the two met, "My wife Ellie tells me you're somebody famous, but what's your handicap, pal?" Tom soon realized Baryshnikov was no hacker; he had a perfect swing and owned some of the finest clubs available.

Baryshnikov had a great time that day. Here were two guys who weren't going to fawn over Misha's fame, but just enjoy playing golf with him. After that first round, Dennis invited all of us for lunch at Gratzi, one of his restaurants on Main Street. Tom had to decline. On the way to Gratzi, Dennis and I stopped by the offices of the Main Street Association and surprised his wife, Ellie. She screamed when she saw Baryshnikov at the doorway. While eating at Gratzi, Misha looked up on the ledge and asked, "What are those?" Dennis responded: "Those are my pre-embargoed Cuban cigars." Misha gave him a look that indicated he appreciated such luxuries. "How about we enjoy a few on the course tomorrow?," suggested Dennis.

The next day Misha played golf on the U-M's Radrick course with Dennis and two gentlemen from Toyota, Chuck Gulash and Jim Griffin. Toyota's local Ann Arbor operation was a generous supporter of our family programming.

On the night before Misha left town for the play's next stop on the tour, Dennis hosted a remarkable dinner in the wine cellar below the Chop House in Misha's honor. Eleven of us joined Dennis, Ellie, Niki, and Alisha Serras and Misha for Kobe beef, lobster flown in from God knows where, and exquisite wines. Before leaving, Dennis and Misha exchanged cell phone numbers.

A few weeks after the Ann Arbor run, in the second performance of a six-performance run at the Kennedy Center in Washington on November 11, one of Misha's fellow actors, Gregory Mitchell, collapsed on stage from a heart attack and died several days later. The Kennedy Center run continued with a substitute actor, but the rest of the tour was cancelled. Misha called Dennis, told him that the tour was coming to an end prematurely, and made a suggestion. "When we were out on the Radrick course, you said something about you and the boys going down to Florida to play golf for a week in December," said Misha. "Since I'm free now, is there any chance I can come down and join you guys?" "Of course," said Dennis. Thus began a special relationship between Mikhail Baryshnikov and the entire Serras family.[4]

The five separate performances making up the Arab World Music Festival from October 2004 through April 2005 were all very well received. We closed out the series thinking we'd done a fine job of choosing a diverse lineup of performers showcasing both the venerable traditions of Arab music and culture and what cutting-edge composers and musicians were doing to take those traditions in new directions.

We felt prepared and inspired to begin planning a similar festival for the 2005–06 season that would feature music from Africa and the African diaspora. And beyond that we envisioned festivals focused on music from the Americas and then from Asia and the Indian Subcontinent. The success of the Arab World Music Festival rested to a great extent on partnering with people and organizations in our regional Arab community, and we knew that our subsequent festivals would thrive if we could rely on similar relationships with the associated communities in our area. I had initiated some of the connections with these communities, and knew I could trust Ben Johnson, his staff, and many others at UMS to maintain communication. The secret was to approach our relationships in such a way that the people in each community we worked with would come to know that UMS was seeking to learn and grow and do the right thing by their community.

We were thrilled in November 2004 when we received notice that UMS was one of six arts organizations in the United States to receive an inaugural Wallace Excellence Award "to build public participation in our programs." Of the six recipients, UMS was the only university presenter. The award came with a grant of $1 million, set up as an endowment challenge. We were successful in matching it. We then pooled these UMS funds with endowments from all the other U-M units, which had an excellent track record of growth. This good fortune would prove not to be a one-off occurrence: in July 2006 we received another challenge grant, this time a $750,000 award from the Doris Duke Charitable Foundation's new Leading College and University Presenter Program, the purpose of which was "to support our artistic programs over the long term." All of

Celebrating the Africa Festival at the U-M Alumni Association Headquarters during the 2005-06 season.

us at UMS felt great pride and satisfaction in being recognized this way by two major national foundations. The grants testified to how far we had come as an organization and held much promise for the future.

Although we had put a great deal of energy into our work with the Arab community over the preceding year or so, we had been nurturing our relationships with the African American community all along as well, and 2005 saw the development of new relationships in Ann Arbor and Detroit. Catherine Blackwell, a legendary teacher and leader in the African American community in Detroit, hosted a backyard dinner at her home in July where our staff members were introduced to about 100 black community leaders in Detroit. At that event, we were excited to announce the upcoming festival featuring music of the African diaspora.

We were proud of the work Ben Johnson had been doing to partner with Detroit arts organizations and the Detroit Public Schools. Under Ben's leadership, we had developed significant projects in Ann Arbor and Detroit with the Sphinx Organization and Mosaic Youth Theatre. As noted earlier, the Sphinx Organization, founded in 1997 by U-M alumnus Aaron Dworkin, works to address the underrepresentation of people of color in classical music. Mosaic Youth Theatre, founded in 1992 by Ann Arbor native Rick Sperling, is an afterschool program for kids with talent; the name "Mosaic" was intended to represent the diversity of the cultures that the program tapped into within Detroit. We had also built successful partnerships with the Paul Robeson Academy, Renaissance High School, Martin Luther King High School, and Cass Technical High School.

The third Royal Shakespeare Company residency was coming up fast and with it we faced a new challenge. The University had made it clear at the end of the 2003 residency to both UMS and the RSC that, given financial challenges U-M was facing, its level of support for the third residency would be cut 83 percent. This meant that UMS would need to negotiate much more vigorously with the RSC and seek new sources of external funding for the residency. Recognizing that UMS had taken on a fair amount of risk in both the first and second residencies—supporting lesser-known Shakespeare works in the first and the creation from scratch of the Rushdie stage adaptation in the second—I was eager to land some sure winners for the third and final residency. We needed sure winners not only to assure a robust box office but also to attract the external funding we would need to offset the substantial decline in U-M support. I asked Michael Boyd, now the artistic director of the RSC, to provide us with some great Shakespeare titles and some certified stars. He did not disappoint. "How about *Antony and Cleopatra, The Tempest, and Julius Caesar* as the plays?," Michael responded. "And Patrick Stewart and Harriet Walter as the stars?" I couldn't have been happier.

We were planning a residency with even more connections to a variety of programs within and outside of the university than the previous residencies. It would also span a longer period of time—20 days—and include more performances. Each of the three plays would be performed seven times. All of this would cost money. In fact, we expected the Royal Shakespeare Company residency of 2006 to be the largest and most expensive project undertaken by UMS in its history. The direct costs of the residency were estimated to exceed $2 million, and total costs, with overhead and the value of in-kind contributions included, to go well over $3 million. We expected income from ticket sales to cover no more than 70 percent of the direct costs, and probably less. In our fundraising, we left no stones unturned, seeking contributions and sponsorships from corporations, foundations, government agencies, the University of Michigan, and individuals. We submitted a grant proposal to the Michigan Economic Development Corporation (MEDC) under UMS auspices, arguing that if Ann Arbor's quality of life and cultural amenities could convince corporations to locate or relocate their businesses or offices in southeast Michigan, then an investment in those amenities would be an investment in the region's economic vitality. Our partners in the MEDC proposal were Ann Arbor SPARK, the Ann Arbor Convention and Visitors Bureau, and U-M's Tech Transfer Office.

Besides having a different funding scenario than the two previous residencies, the one in 2006 would occur in the fall instead of the spring. This shift in scheduling would give us more time for planning and fundraising, and it opened up new possibilities for involving the company with football. For the residencies in 2001 and 2003, Lloyd Carr, the football coach, had invited the cast to come down and witness practice. That was all they could do because it was spring. A residency in the fall meant they could be involved during an actual game, and I knew Coach Carr could arrange for the cast to have access to the field. That got me thinking.

During the summer of 2006 I sent a message to Patrick Stewart that went like this: "Dear Mr. Stewart, I'd like to offer you a leading role, center stage, in the largest theatre in the round in the United States of America. Are you interested?" He replied with an "absolutely" and asked what I had in mind. "I'd like for you to conduct the Michigan Marching Band during halftime of the Michigan home game on November 4th in front of 110,000 people." He was all in! I told the Michigan Marching Band that Patrick Stewart had agreed to be conductor, and they proceeded to plan a whole halftime show around it.

Once the RSC cast arrived in Ann Arbor on October 22, the University of Michigan's Power Center became a beehive of intense activity. The 21-performance run was one of the most complex theatrical projects ever undertaken by a presenter working with a nonresident company. As many as 70 people worked backstage over the course of the residency to mount the three plays. The 70 Royal Shakespeare Company members who made up the entourage from Stratford-upon-Avon, including actors, musicians, directors, technical crew, producers, administrators, and educators, made appearances all over southeast Michigan when they weren't at the Power

The 2006 Royal Shakespeare Company residency included three titles on the Power Center stage and Ken hosting actors Harriet Walter and Patrick Stewart at Michigan Stadium where Patrick conducted the Michigan Marching Band in the largest 'theater-in-the-round' in the U.S. during a U-M football game. November 4, 2006.

Center. Beyond the plays themselves, there were 40 public educational events, three exhibitions, and more than 100 private educational events.

A local Gallery Crawl featured a costume exhibit at the Ann Arbor District Library. An exhibition of photos and other memorabilia on the three RSC plays was on display at the Hatcher Graduate Library. Teachers in local schools participated in preparatory workshops followed by in-school RSC activities. Theater professor Malcolm Tulip interviewed lead actors Harriet Walter and Patrick Stewart on campus. RSC members led a *Julius Caesar* workshop with young actors from the Mosaic Youth Theatre two hours before the RSC actors themselves would be performing the play on the Power Center stage. In Detroit, 70 students from Cass Technical, University Prep, and Renaissance High Schools worked with RSC assistant director Gemma Fairlie and professional area actors in a six-week RSC project called Playback! to learn *Julius Caesar*; the project culminated in a production of *Julius Caesar* by the students for their families and friends.

From across the state of Michigan, over 3,000 high school students attended the three Royal Shakespeare Company dress rehearsals. Some of them traveled from as far away as the Interlochen Arts Academy—a four-hour drive from Ann Arbor. Hundreds more were impacted by the educational events happening in their classrooms, libraries, and theaters. UMS had worked for more than a year with over 40 partners throughout southeast Michigan to plan and carry out all the residency events with partners that included 25 units of the University of Michigan and 50 individual U-M faculty members.

In the middle of it all, on Saturday, November 4, was the football game between Michigan and Ball State. At halftime, the score was 24 to 12, with Michigan leading. The Michigan Marching Band took the field and played several theme songs from television shows, including *Hawaii 5-O*, *Gilligan's Island*, and *Dallas*. Before the final number, Patrick Stewart, introduced as Captain Jean-Luc Picard, Patrick's character in *Star Trek*, and wearing his Michigan fleece, mounted the ladder. Patrick raised the baton and the band proceeded to play the theme from *Star Trek, the Next Generation*. The crowd of 110,000 went nuts. For the second part of the performance, he turned around, and from out of the press box, Carl Grapentine's voice declared, "Captain, in two weeks we go to Columbus; what are your orders?" Holding up his microphone, Captain Jean-Luc Picard gave his command to the Wolverines: "Boldly go forth and beat the Buckeyes;

make it so Number One."[5] Michigan went on to win that day's surprisingly close game against Ball State, 34 to 26.

Attendance at the twenty-one regular performances of *Antony and Cleopatra*, *Julius Caesar*, and *The Tempest* was just shy of 27,000 people. They came from 39 states and four countries to see the plays. UMS made 2,500 discounted tickets available to students for the regular performances, many of which were purchased by students enrolled in the 13 for-credit U-M courses created specifically because of the RSC residency.

Ticket-sales income ended up covering 65 percent of the direct costs. The remainder of the residency's direct costs were covered by contributions from a wide variety of entities, including DTE Energy, Pfizer, Northwest Airlines, the Power Foundation, and the Michigan Council for Arts and Cultural Affairs. An important source of support came from the Michigan Economic Development Corporation, which sponsored the *Julius Caesar* plays and the November 2–4 Business Familiarization Trip, in which 10 corporate executives visited Ann Arbor to see Shakespeare and attend the U-M football game. James Epolito, CEO of MEDC, was quoted as saying that its sponsorship was the "best return-on-investment" of any MEDC sponsorship. Two companies located in Michigan as a result of participating in the Shakespeare weekend. Mary Kramer, publisher of *Crain's Detroit Business*, wrote in the November 13th issue, "The MEDC hit a home run with its investment in Shakespeare."

In all its aspects, the 2006 RSC residency was extraordinarily successful for UMS. It strengthened our partnerships and connections with the community and throughout the university. Financially, we had been able to compensate for the university's cut in its support by finding new types of support from corporations and the state—an expansion of our funding base that would help smooth out the bumps ahead.

Shortly after the 2006 residency, Ralph and I were over in London to begin conversations with the RSC about what the next stage of our relationship might look like now that we had completed the three residencies that were part of our initial agreement. We were leaving the meeting when Michael Boyd and Jeremy Adams said they had something else they ought to tell us. "Do you know anything about The Ohio State University?" Ralph and I looked at each other, returned to the office, and took a seat. Michael and Jeremy told us that Les Wexner, a businessman, OSU board member, and major OSU donor, had begun to talk with them. Les Wexner's wife,

Abigail, was cochairing the committee organizing the Bicentennial of the City of Columbus; they were interested in getting the Royal Shakespeare Company involved in their literacy campaign. Michael and Jeremy told us they were not intending to have performances at Ohio State, but they were beginning a new and potentially significant relationship with another Midwest university and Midwest community.

Ralph and I found ourselves in an interesting position. On the one hand, we were thrilled for our colleagues at the RSC that they were building a new relationship with a major donor willing to provide generous support. On the other hand, we were disappointed that the University of Michigan's pull-back in funding had apparently been interpreted as a sign of declining support, and we were wondering what the relationship with Ohio State might lead to.

On February 7, 2007, I saw Professor Patricia Gurin talking with colleagues over lunch at Zanzibar Restaurant on South State Street. I'd known Pat and her husband, Jerry, for more than 40 years and wanted to say hello, so I stopped by her table. After exchanging our greetings, Pat introduced me to those at the table I didn't know and then began thanking me for all the work UMS had done over the years to promote diversity. This message had some relevance for everyone at the table, because the lunch meeting had been convened to discuss responses to the passage of Michigan Proposition 2 a few months previously, a turn of events that appeared to outlaw all forms of affirmative action in the state. I left the restaurant feeling buoyed, with no expectation that anything more would come from the exchange.

Two days later, I was copied on an email that Pat Gurin sent to the two top officers at the university, President Mary Sue Coleman and Provost Teresa Sullivan. It bowled me over as I read it. In short, Pat's letter thoroughly validated all the work we had done over the previous two decades to make UMS more inclusive, to reach out to underrepresented groups, and to use the arts to generate understanding and bring people together. Its force was amplified by who it was coming from: Pat had conducted the research supporting U-M's contention that having a diverse student body brings significant positive educational outcomes and impacts students' learning and behavior for their lifetimes, and she had been a tireless supporter of the university's affirmative action policies. I couldn't think of anyone with greater credibility on the issue of diversity.

In her letter, Pat said that she had attended UMS events before 1987 and that they had changed radically since that time. "Attending events at Hill or the Power Center is now a totally different cultural experience," she wrote, "both because of the many rich, cultural representations UMS brings to the stage and because of the diverse audiences that now flock to UMS events." Noting that "some particular events draw huge numbers of people from particular ethnic/racial communities," she said that "UMS has obviously found ways to reach out and collaborate with specific cultural communities in the state."

The letter went on to make the point that connecting with and programming for diverse communities wasn't the only contribution UMS had made to diversity. UMS, she said, had also exposed "the majority population to the arts of many peoples, some of which reflect historical and some contemporary expressions of the arts from many parts of the world." She lauded how UMS had also "effectively exposed school children in our surrounding communities and in Detroit to this rich array of cultural experiences." She summed up the whole tribute with this gracious conclusion: "I know of no institution that projects our commitment to diversity and connects to the wider community as compellingly as the UMS. It is a jewel for the University." To say this made my day is putting it lightly.

Although we could celebrate our accomplishments in 2007, the recession of 2008 brought a period of difficulty and struggle, as it did for many educational institutions, nonprofits, businesses, and families. We suffered declines in corporate and university support and in attendance. The hit to our finances required us to let go of five of our staff members and impose temporary salary reductions. But our growth and evolution over the previous decades had made the organization nothing if not strong and resilient. We weathered the storm and came out looking for new challenges.

Notes

1. Mr. Oyelowo's performance in the plays won him critical acclaim and the 2001 Ian Charleson Award for best performance by an actor under 30 in a classical play.

2. The residency proved to be a boon to Michael Boyd's career as well. His work as director was masterful. Later that year he received the coveted Olivier Award in Britain for "Best Director" for his work on the history plays. That unprecedented achievement elevated him in the eyes of the company and he became the RSC's artistic director in 2003.

3. Attorney and UMS board member Alice Irani had taken on the task of securing visas for the large number of cast members, many with non-Western names. We were worried about delays given the heightened security measures put in place after 9/11. But the visas were all approved within 10 days of Alice submitting the forms in late December—attesting to the quality of Alice's work and her good relationships with State Department officials.

4. Sadly, Dennis died on January 30, 2019. Misha and friends created a video tribute to Dennis that they sent to the Serras family.

5. The Wolverines couldn't quite follow through on Captain Picard's command. In one of the greatest games ever played between Ohio State and Michigan, the Buckeyes won 42 to 39, securing the #1 ranking for the season. To make matters worse, the legendary former Michigan coach Bo Schembechler died the day before the game. However, Bo had been able to see the RSC perform *Antony and Cleopatra*, the first live professional performance of a Shakespeare play he had ever experienced, and to thoroughly enjoy conversing with the actors Finbar Lynch and John Light during a preperformance reception.

seven
Going Renegade

Once we had eased out of the belt-tightening period that followed the financial crisis of 2008, we at UMS were ready to yet again move into new territory. Having built a loyal following and gained a stellar reputation, we could take more risks in what we presented. Continuing in the direction of expanding our aesthetic boundaries, we significantly increased the number of presentations that challenged our audiences.

The concern for any presenter in offering cutting-edge work is that audiences will stay away because it is not familiar. The fear is that prospective attendees will look at the program and think, "I'm not going because I don't know it." It's a valid concern because many people aren't particularly adventurous by nature and want to stay within their comfort zones. But people also like to see themselves as knowing insiders, as being abreast of current trends. With that in mind, we deliberately worked on shifting the frame so that when people saw something on the program they didn't know they said, "I want to go to that *because* I don't know it." We wanted to be seen as having chosen performers who should not be missed precisely because they had not achieved mass appeal.

By 2010 we had become increasingly successful at doing that. Our audiences came to expect that UMS was going to do more than just present a Berlin Philharmonic, or a Wynton Marsalis, or a Yo-Yo Ma; yes, we continued to present such performers, but people expected new artists as well. They wanted to come and not be quite sure what they were going to experience. Increasingly, enough people made that leap for us to feel secure in offering programming with the potential to disorient or disrupt or even disturb.

In order for us to be aware of the artists and performers who were doing best at transcending boundaries and creating new aesthetic standards, we had to get out into the world and experience them. Staff members had to go to the Edinburgh Festival, or Amsterdam, or Barcelona. One important change for us (thanks to our donors!) was that we began to have the resources to support that kind of travel.

We saw our sharpening focus on cutting-edge work as entirely consistent with our affiliation with a truly great university. The academic enterprise is about stretching people and enabling them to grow, and this was exactly what we were doing in the artistic realm by making the works we presented be educational experiences.

But to fully realize the possibilities entailed in being a university presenter, we had to create even more opportunities for students and professors to work with our artists and engage with the works they performed. It was time, we thought, to build on our success in integrating our presenting with the educational mission of the university and take it to a new level. To do this, we needed additional funding.

In 2009, not yet out of the shadow of the period of austerity brought on by the recession, we had dedicated quite a bit of effort to developing proposals that might yield significant funding from major foundations. In these proposals, we highlighted our track record of collaboration with the University of Michigan over the previous decade. Our residency work in dance, theater, and music had gained heightened visibility and praise from the field, thanks in large part to the outstanding work of Ben Johnson, who had so brilliantly led our education and community engagement efforts, and the investments we had made in our education program, from the annual grant we received from the University, had clearly benefitted many U-M students.[1]

All this work and preparation paid off. On January 7, 2010, a press release announced that UMS would receive a three-and-a-half-year grant of $600,000 from the Andrew W. Mellon Foundation. It was one of three at that level that the foundation awarded, the other two going to Krannert Center at the University of Illinois and Cal Performances at the University of California at Berkeley. Mellon decided to give significant grants to three presenters of classical music at major research universities that were also committed to deepening their engagement with the academic units. In effect, Mellon was saying that "we will support your efforts if you are serious about integrating what you put on stage with what goes on in the classroom." The Mellon grant carried few strings, enabling us to fund educational programs, commissions, and performances—the full gamut of teaching, research, and service. It had a profound effect on the way in which we partnered with the University of Michigan.

That summer, we learned that we had received another major education-focused grant—a Creative Campus Innovations Grant, funded by the Doris Duke Charitable Foundation, from the Association of Performing Arts Presenters. When I took the call from APAP president Sandra Gibson, she told me that UMS had received "a perfect score" on the proposal from a panel of peers. In my experience that had never happened before. I immediately called UMS's masterful proposal writer Lisa Murray to congratulate her.

This grant would support the Medical School's Medical Arts Program, which was dedicated to integrating the arts into the medical curriculum. It had been founded in the mid-2000s by U-M faculty member Joel Howell and his colleagues in the medical school, Sanjay Saint and Jim Stanley. Joel, Sanjay, and Jim believed that medical students exposed to musical, theatrical, literary, and visual arts while in school would become better doctors because that exposure would help them build essential but otherwise overlooked skills such as empathy, awareness of social context, and comfort with ambiguity. Previously supported only with the resources Joel, Sanjay, and Jim could scrape together, the Medical Arts Program was formalized and greatly expanded with the $200,000 infusion from the APAP grant.

As UMS changed as an organization, so too did my role as its leader. With a first-rate, dedicated staff, diminished worries about funding, and good relationships with the UMS board and with University and community leaders, I felt less of a need to guide the direction of the organization. It had become, to a great extent, a ship that sailed itself. As a result, I was able to devote more time to the field and to mentoring. I could give back to the colleagues and institutions that helped me along the way, and I could offer my expertise to help advance the causes I cared about. For the most part, this meant serving on boards of directors and as an officer in some cases. Among the boards on which I served were those of the Association of Performing Arts Professionals (vice chair), Chamber Music America (chair), International Society for the Performing Arts, Classical Action/Performing Arts Against AIDS, Interlochen Center for the Arts, National

Arts Strategies (chair), and the Cultural Alliance of Southeast Michigan, now called CultureSource.

I could also do more things that were just plain fun. One example: on the occasion of the 2010 U-M Spring Commencement at Michigan Stadium, I served as "color commentator" beside well-known Detroit anchorman Huel Perkins for the Big Ten Network's coverage of the event. Michigan Radio's executive director and U-M's director of Michigan Public Media Steve Schram had invited me to serve in this role given that I had a long history with U-M and had some experience with radio. The festivities got off to a rousing start when UMS intern and graduating U-M soprano Mary Martin sang the National Anthem. When she got to "and the land of the free," she took "free" up an octave and held it for what seemed forever as the whole stadium erupted in applause and cheers. President Obama then delivered the commencement address and received an honorary degree. I had worked with four of the six other honorary degree recipients in some capacity. They were Jean Campbell, the cofounder of U-M's Center for the Education of Women and the person in whose home I lived the first summer of my UMS tenure; jazz legend Ornette Coleman, whom UMS presented in the 2003–04 season; NPR journalist Susan Stamberg, whom I met during my Washington days and invited to interview Isaac Stern for the 2000 Ford Honors Program; and former MIT president Charles Vest, who had become U-M provost shortly after I arrived and with whom I had stayed in touch over the years.

We had been saddened not to be able to bring the Royal Shakespeare Company back to Ann Arbor after their third performance residency in 2006. Part of the reason was that the relationship between the RSC and Ohio State that Michael Boyd and Jeremy Adams told us about in 2006 had indeed blossomed and led to something significant. By 2009, supported with funding from Abigail and Les Wexner and others, Ohio State had formalized a partnership with the Royal Shakespeare Company that had the company coming to Ohio to lead educational activities for schoolchildren across the state. Through this partnership, Ohio State was also supporting the company's tours in the United States, which included the "Cycle of Kings" tetralogy consisting of the four other history plays of Shakespeare that were not presented in Ann Arbor.

However, the University of Michigan was able to bring the Royal Shakespeare Company back to Michigan in 2010 (and then again in 2012)

Ken provides color commentary with Detroit TV news anchor Huel Perkins for the Big Ten Network's coverage at the 2010 U-M spring commencement featuring President Obama as the speaker and honorary degree recipient.

for what we called a "creative residency." Way back at the time of the RSC's first residency at U-M in 2001, Lee Bollinger had set aside some cash in a discretionary fund in the Office of the President with the idea of bringing Michael Boyd to the campus as a visiting professor. That had not happened in the intervening years because once Michael became the artistic director of the RSC in 2003 he had almost no time for that sort of thing. With the money now transferred to the English Department under Ralph Williams's auspices, Ralph and Assistant to the President Gary Krenz began plotting how to bring the RSC back, even without Michael Boyd.

The arrangement Gary and Ralph Williams worked out with the RSC's Michael Boyd and Jeremy Adams was that a "creative team" from the RSC, made up of playwrights, directors, key actors, and dramaturges, would all come to the University of Michigan and spend about 10 days on campus, working on new plays or adaptations of existing plays. The goal would be to develop and fine-tune the scripts of the plays. Throughout the residency, the creative team would work with U-M faculty members who had expertise in subjects pertinent to the plays. U-M students in theater and music would also participate in the development of the plays, working alongside the renowned RSC playwrights and directors.

Although I was helpful in negotiating and making other connections, I wasn't heavily involved in planning the residency because it wasn't a UMS project. The initiative came from the Office of the President and English Department, and Gary Krenz and Ralph Williams were in charge of making it happen. However, I did play a useful role in finding an ideal housing arrangement for the company by making a deal with Bob Dolan, the dean of the business school. (I had met Bob around 2000 when the university was recruiting him to head the business school. He was ready to come, but his wife, Kathleen, not so much. I had been assigned the ambassadorial role of persuading the arts-focused Kathleen that Ann Arbor would be a great place to live. I succeeded.) When I asked Bob for help with housing the RSC, he said, "Absolutely, Ken, just have them stay here." We both agreed that having them stay in his brand-new business school was a terrific idea. The entire company could live, eat, and do all their work in the Ross School of Business Executive Residence. They could have the use of workrooms and the school's Blau Auditorium, where they could do the readings of the plays.

The 10 days of creative work in March 2010 were intense and productive for all involved. The company brought three plays to work on: *Cardenio*, a play attributed to Shakespeare and his contemporary John Fletcher that was performed in 1613 but for which no text existed; a play by RSC associate Robert Edgar on Lancelot Andrewes's work on bringing the King James Bible to publication; and a play by Helen Edmundson about the life of Sor Juana Inés de la Cruz, a South American nun, playwright, and essayist who lived in the 1600s. With Ralph Williams playing a key role through it all, students and faculty provided input and knowledge that helped inform the evolution of the plays in their preperformance stages. In addition to developing the scripts of the plays, the participants worked on direction, acting, staging, choreography, incidental music, and other aspects of production. The LAByrinth theater company from New York, with a highly diverse set of actors, was invited to come on board and participate. During the course of the residency, three public discussions were held, one on each of the plays; members of the RSC creative team gave a public lecture; and Ralph Williams joined with RSC members to hold a public discussion on the more general topic of treating the Bible as literature.

At the Ross School, Bob assigned Lynnette Iannance to oversee things. She was British and very excited about the project. She soon discovered that the Royal Shakespeare Company's award-winning director Gregory Doran was the same person with whom she had participated in a fourth-grade pantomime back in England, he working backstage, she acting onstage. I loved hearing that this had happened; you always wonder if things are going to work and then suddenly, without your knowing it, something magical happens. Add to this Lynnette's motivation to do whatever she could to make the thing work, and it was just marvelous.

The RSC members loved the hospitality they were shown; it was really a feather in the cap of the business school. The company viewed the residency as an immensely valuable creative opportunity, and this helped maintain the University of Michigan's strong relationship with the Royal Shakespeare Company, ensuring that a second creative residency would occur in 2012.[2] By collaborating together, UMS, the U-M President's Office, the English Department, and the Ross School of Business pioneered a new way of having a theater company engage with faculty and students in the process of making art.

In the summer of 2011, the deepening relationship between Les Wexner and the Royal Shakespeare Company was on conspicuous display in New York City. Wexner, who had a home in Warwickshire, 16 miles from Stratford-upon-Avon, had approached the leadership of the RSC with the open-ended question "What do you need?" and the RSC had given a ready answer—"A New York season." The result was a rare six-week residency at the Park Avenue Armory, under the auspices of the Lincoln Center Festival. The Wexners funded the construction of a stage built specifically for the performances (the Scarlet and Gray stage of The Ohio State University). Essentially, a Shakespearean theater was built inside the Park Avenue Armory, and it was just stunning. When Ralph Williams and I met with Michael Boyd in his office at the Armory during the residency, Michael made it clear that the gift from the Wexners had come with the suggestion that the RSC not bring performances to the University of Michigan for a while. Creative residencies, though, were just fine.

Earlier in 2011, I attended the annual Association of Performing Arts Professionals conference in January in New York City, as I always had done. Penny came with me this time, planning to attend some of the conference sessions and social events and also visit her flute colleagues at the Flute

Ken accepting APAP's Fan Taylor Award after Colleen Jennings-Roggensack introduces him. January 2011.

Center of New York. APAP gives four awards each year at this conference: the Award of Merit for achievement in the performing arts; the Sidney R. Yates Advocacy Award for outstanding advocacy on behalf of the performing arts; the William Dawson Award for Programmatic Excellence and sustained achievement in programming; and the Fan Taylor Distinguished Service Award for exemplary service to the field of professional presenting. The recipients of the first three are known to all in advance; the Fan Taylor awardee is kept secret. Among the previous winners of the Fan Taylor award were colleagues whose contributions to the field had truly inspired me: Philip Bither (2009), Colleen Jennings-Roggensack (2007), John Killacky (2004), Olga Garay (2003), Susie Farr (2002), Jacqueline Davis (2001), Jerry Yoshitomi (1992), and Halsey North (1988).

As a donor to APAP's Bill Dawson Endowment Fund, I had a reserved table at the Awards Luncheon to which I had invited APAP colleagues, foundation friends, and UMS National Council members living in New York. I had bought a luncheon ticket for Penny, but she was absent. I tried to call her to remind her of the luncheon but got no response. At the point in the program when the Fan Taylor awardee would be announced, Colleen Jennings-Roggensack came to the podium to do the honors. As is customary, Colleen built up the suspense, providing only obscure clues to the awardee's identity. As her introduction moved along, she revealed clues that let me and others know that I would be the recipient. I was thrilled, but also disappointed that Penny was not there for the occasion. As I came to the stage, I was surprised to see our son Matt and his one-and-a-half-year-old son, Alex, approach the stage as well. Then it dawned on me: they were in on the secret and had flown in from California with Matt's wife, Renee. And I realized that Penny wasn't at my table because she was orchestrating Matt, Renee, and Alex's arrival at the hotel so that I wouldn't know about it. I was deeply moved not only by receiving the award but by having my family there to celebrate with me.

About a month after the conference, APAP asked me, as the 2011 Fan Taylor awardee, to share 10 principles about effective leadership that could be published in the association's magazine, *Inside Arts*. By this time, I had very clear ideas about what practices had worked for me and which I attributed to the success of UMS. The difficulty was distilling them down to 10 distinct things. Here is an abridged version of what APAP published:

> **Have an overarching relationship policy that guides your work.** Mine is "Everybody In, Nobody Out," which I learned from my mentor, the late Patrick Hayes, founder of the Washington Performing Arts Society. This policy of inclusion, I believe, was key to our organizational transformation.
>
> **Get out of the office.** Go to where people are—their homes, stores, community centers, churches, offices—to sustain existing relationships and build new ones. Twice a month, for example, I walk the halls of the U-M Fleming Administration Building, connecting with university executive officers and their staffs in a way I never could if I depended on formal appointments.
>
> **Create authentic partnerships by practicing Sharon King's four relationship principles—communication, cooperation, vulnerability, reciprocity**. Vulnerability and reciprocity are the most important and most challenging because they require humility and putting yourself in your partner's shoes.
>
> **Learn people's names and their correct pronunciations; then practice what you learn.** A great way to practice is to introduce people to one another and say something interesting about each person when you do.

Hire people of proven or potential talent and then build a great team with them. Together with your team, create an inspiring mission and ambitious goals and then give your team the opportunity to succeed, individually and collectively.

Learn from the best. When I entered the field, I randomly asked presenters and managers who they considered to be the top presenters in the country. I sought those who were consistently named, and they became my mentors and good friends.

Be willing to adapt. If you're continually learning, you'll be exposed to valuable perspectives and fresh ideas that will enable you to stay ahead of the game and make the changes that will keep your organization successful.

Share your passion and enthusiasm. I'm excited to be able to work in the performing arts field at a respected organization in a remarkably supportive community with talented staff members and dedicated volunteers. I share this enthusiasm wherever I can and invite people to join in.

Serve the field. The field needs good people to serve on grant panels, conference committees, boards of directors, and other volunteer positions. I can tell you from experience that the return on the time you invest pays off significantly in professional development opportunities, benefits to your organization, and new friendships.

Surround yourself with young people. Give time to interns, students, younger staff members, and emerging leaders. Listen to them and share your knowledge and experience, and be kind. Who knows? Some day you may be working for one of them!

In 2011, Programming Director Michael Kondziolka began thinking about putting together a new series at UMS. In keeping with the way UMS had been evolving as a presenter, he wanted to shake things up a bit. He wanted to go for the unfamiliar, the unknown, the unexpected—different kinds of venues, completely different or deeper experiences, unusual lengths, provocative subject matter, different languages, or no language at all. He wanted us to take risks—the kinds of risks that other presenters might shy away from but which we were ready to embrace. He had my support and that of the M-Team to continue developing this approach.

What's key in developing the concept for something new like this is the name you give it. After much discussion, we settled on the name *rene-*

gade. The word, as it's defined in English, carries a negative connotation of betrayal, but it also suggests rebellion and unconventionality. It was those latter two senses that we wanted to bring into play with the name "Renegade Series."

In an interview, when Michael was asked why he chose the name, he had this to say:

> Ultimately we wanted to choose a word that hasn't been overused, a word that maybe made people feel both a little bit curious and a little bit uncomfortable. I like the word [renegade], because it toggles between the artists, their artistic output, and the audience. What does it mean if you're an audience member who chooses to go to these sorts of events? Are you a little bit of a renegade? Are you taking a risk? How do you feel about taking that risk, and what do you get out of taking that risk? As consumers of the arts—as listeners and observers—it is the moments when we take risks, or step into something that we have no idea what it is, and are completely bowled over and changed, that matter.

When you launch a new series, you want the first work you present to set the tone for everything that comes after. Michael had in mind something that seemed perfect: the five-hour Philip Glass opera *Einstein on the Beach*, written in 1975 and premiered at the Avignon Festival in 1976. *Einstein* was staged in several other European cities and New York in 1976, then remounted in 1984 in Brooklyn. A reworked version was produced in 1988, and a revival of the original toured in 1992. Not including three derived productions—"opera-installations" in Germany in 2001 and 2005 and a concert version in 2007—the opera had not been staged since 1992. It was not from lack of trying: director Robert Wilson, composer Philip Glass, choreographer Lucinda Childs, and their producer Linda Brumbach of Pomegranate Arts had been trying to bring the opera back to life since 2000, and even got as far as a commission with the New York City Opera for 2009, but these efforts had failed to materialize for various reasons.

Michael and I knew about Linda's stymied ambitions for *Einstein on the Beach* and offered to remount the opera in January 2012 as the premiere event of the new Renegade Series. To convince Linda that it was the right thing to do, we pointed out that remounting the opera at a university would benefit many students and faculty members and that U-M's aspir-

Einstein on the Beach director Robert Wilson, composer Philip Glass, and cho-reographer Lucinda Childs at the Penny Stamps Lecture during the opera's remounting under UMS auspices. January 15, 2012.

ing artists would soak up every opportunity to work with Philip Glass and Robert Wilson and Lucinda Childs and the members of the cast. Everyone agreed that it should happen.

For financial support, we invited Maxine and Stuart Frankel, longtime friends of the visual and performing arts programs at the University of Michigan, to consider becoming the leading supporters of our Renegade Series.[3] Believing that a national leader in the presentation of the perform-ing arts must push the boundaries of knowledge forward by supporting new works, remounting important past works, and providing a venue and funding for artists to create, the Frankels established the Creative Ven-tures Leadership Fund, with a multiyear challenge grant to support the Renegade Series. The Mellon and Knight Foundations were major con-tributors to the match as were the Power Foundation and Brian and Mary Campbell in honor of Herbert Amster.

For additional support, we turned once again to the Michigan Eco-nomic Development Corporation. Because of the recognized success of the MEDC grant supporting the 2006 RSC residency, we were in the good graces of MEDC and could easily make the case that the distinctive event would draw audiences from throughout the United States and beyond, demonstrate the high quality of life in Ann Arbor, and possibly figure in business's decisions about where to locate. Since the signature program of the MEDC was a campaign, called "Pure Michigan," that highlighted the many recreational, cultural, and educational assets of the state in award-winning television, radio, and print advertising, we gave the name Pure Michigan Renegade to our program for its first year once the MEDC grant was confirmed. At the same time UMS was gathering support for the remount in Ann Arbor, Linda was obtaining support of a core group of performing arts presenting organizations around the world who would eventually present the work.

Sixty-seven artists, crew, and staff members connected with the production came to Ann Arbor and most stayed for much of the month of January, working at the Power Center. Dennis Dahlmann made it possible for the whole company to stay at a deeply discounted rate at his Campus Inn, a full-service hotel only one long block from the Power Center. The UMS staff, our outstanding production and artist services team, and our dedicated union stagehands—who love challenges like this—were all put at the company's service. Thirty-four local stagehands and theater technicians were hired to assist with the remounting process. It was expensive and risky, but UMS had evolved to the point that such a project should be something we were poised to do.

The four-week-long remounting residency, led by creators Robert Wilson and Philip Glass, was rich with activity. Philip Glass facilitated a Saturday morning physics session. A standing-room-only crowd attended a Penny W. Stamps interview with Wilson and Glass. Altogether, the intellectually rich residency events engaged more than 3,300 students and community members and involved collaboration with numerous campus partners, including the School of Music, Theatre & Dance, the Physics Department, the Ross School of Business, Arts Engine, U-M Health Services, Arts at Michigan, the Institute for the Humanities, the Penny Stamps School of Art & Design, and the U-M Museum of Art. We at UMS were pleased that so many students, faculty, and people in our community were able to benefit from the company's presence.

We were rewarded with three epic performances at the end of the remounting period. UMS board chair and physicist Steve Forrest spoke for many when he later wrote that despite having been an opera buff for 30 years, the performance he experienced left him "awestruck" and altered forever his "perception of what was possible in musical composition." Like Einstein himself, said Steve, *Einstein on the Beach* "completely changed my world." We were proud of what we had helped nurture and satisfied that we had played a key role in bringing this historic opera back to life— probably for the last time with the original creators. Then we sent the production off for a 10-city tour over the next 14 months. It was the perfect way to launch our Renegade Series.

The inaugural season of 2012 also included the "American Mavericks" three-day festival in March with the San Francisco Symphony and Michael Tilson Thomas, with soloists Jeremy Denk, Meredith Monk, Jessye Norman, and Emanuel Ax. We thought it appropriate that the "mavericks" concept fit nicely with the ideas behind the name *renegade.* Tilson Thomas and the San Francisco Symphony performed works by 20th-century musical innovators Charles Ives, John Cage, Henry Cowell, and Lou Harrison as well as new commissioned works by John Adams, Mason Bates, Meredith Monk, and Morton Subotnick. The American Mavericks Festival included a special Friday afternoon youth performance, for which our Youth Education Program created a wonderful teacher resource guide.

We were thrilled when two UMS Renegade productions/presentations were among the "Ten Memorable Classical Performances of 2012" lauded by music writer Alex Ross in an end-of-the-year *New Yorker* article. Ross named the *Einstein on the Beach* remounting in Ann Arbor as his number-one favorite. Number three was the San Francisco Symphony's multiconcert American Mavericks Festival, which was presented only in New York City, San Francisco, and Ann Arbor and would not have happened without UMS's commitment to invest in it and present it.

With generous multiyear support from Maxine and Stuart Frankel, our Renegade Series was assured of a bright future. And it didn't hurt that despite the edginess of what we were presenting, box office results were strong. All told, Pure Michigan Renegade engaged 297 artists for 14 public performances that drew 15,478 audience members from 39 states and 9 countries. In addition, 5,768 students, faculty, and community members participated in the 65 related educational events.

I'd always thought it was important to encourage students to attend our events by offering them discounted tickets. Often we would do this by setting aside some hundreds of tickets that we would sell to students at discounted prices on a first-come, first-served basis. This method worked well, and we figured that the financial impact was more or less neutral—the money we lost from the discounts was made up for by selling more tickets that we otherwise might have. In any case, whatever the bottom-line effect, we were committed to expanding student access.

In 2012, I had the idea of doing it one better. I approached Bert Askwith, the father of UMS National Council member Patti Askwith Kenner and a generous donor to U-M, and proposed that he fund a program that would provide a free ticket to each first-year student at the University of Michigan. Bert was uniquely situated to agree to my proposal. In 1927, when he was a new student at Michigan, Bert came up with the idea of chartering a bus to New York City so that he and other students who lived in the city and found the cost of the train excessive could get back to the city for the holidays. He realized that he could charge the students far less than they would pay for the train and yet clear some profit to help with his college expenses. Thus began Campus Coach Lines, a highly successful charter bus company that Bert founded and led. It paid his way through Michigan and enabled him to give back generously throughout his lifetime. Bert had donated funds that made possible a café and study lounge at the Shapiro Library. He loved students and they loved him. He received hundreds of thank-you notes from U-M students every year. I knew that as a student Bert had had what he considered to be profound experiences at Hill Auditorium and that he would want to make similar experiences possible for students today.

When I made my request, calling the idea "Bert's Ticket," Bert immediately said yes. Nothing could make him happier, he said, than knowing that because of his donation every U-M student could have at least one experience attending a UMS performance.

Bert made a gift to support Bert's Ticket for one year beginning in the 2013–14 season. All that a first-year student had to do was go to our ticket office, show their ID, and say, "I'd like my Bert's ticket." We had no way of knowing what percentage of the many students who took advantage of Bert's Ticket might not have attended a UMS event had a free ticket not been available, but we suspected it was substantial. In any case, we were confident that making it financially easier for students to attend our events through this and other means contributed substantially to a statistic we are very proud of—that students make up nearly a quarter of the UMS audience.

At the end of the 2013–14 season, I invited Bert to consider funding Bert's Ticket for three more years and extending the offer to second-year students as well. He said, "Call me tomorrow at noon, and I'll have an answer." I called the next day at noon. "You know, Ken," he said, "I'm 102, and you're asking me to make a three-year gift. Tell you what—make it two years and you've got a deal." Bert lived to see one of those two years. He died in June 2015 at the age of 104, still working five days a week, eight hours a day. Fortunately for us, Bert's daughter Patti Askwith Kenner kept Bert's Ticket going through her generous support.

The year 2013 was significant for UMS for a number of reasons. In March, the Mellon Foundation awarded us a second three-year grant that allowed us to continue and strengthen the work of integrating arts and education that the first grant in 2010 had funded. As written into the proposal, that work would have three components—all new ways for UMS to achieve educational goals.

The centerpiece of the first component was a new semester-long, three-credit humanities course titled "Engaging Performance." We developed and offered it in partnership with the School of Music, Theatre & Dance and the College of Literature, Science, and the Arts. It was open to any student at U-M without prerequisite. Students in the course attended nine UMS performances representing a wide range of offerings in each genre, attended lectures by visiting artists, and participated in interactive classroom activities. In essence, the performances were the "texts" studied by the students.

The Mellon grant also supported a Faculty Institute, the goal of which was to support efforts to integrate the performing arts into nonarts curricula across many departments. The 15 faculty members selected for the first institute (out of 31 applicants) attended two days of instruction and discussion in May 2014, continued to meet over the next year and receive consultation while developing arts-integrated courses, and then offered those courses for the 2015–16 academic year.

The third component was a faculty advisory group focused on pushing insights in the other direction: from the faculty to UMS. Meeting several times a year with UMS programming and education staff members, the group explored ways of connecting prospective offerings in future seasons with the curricula of existing courses, suggested potential campus partners that had not had previous engagement with UMS, helped our staff members understand the academic planning timetable, and developed strategies for better alignment of UMS activities with curricular goals and themes. Though not in our original proposal, the grant also supported the development of curricular guides that suggest ways of tying each UMS performance to learning objectives and themes in different disciplines.

In June 2013, not long after being awarded the Mellon Foundation grant for arts integration, we learned that Mellon would extend the original grant supporting our classical music program for another three years in the amount of $600,000. We felt honored to be supported so abundantly.

Another major event that year was the centenary of Hill Auditorium. Although Hill Auditorium is owned by the University and overseen by the School of Music, Theatre & Dance—which uses it seven or eight times more than UMS in any given year—UMS seized the opportunity to celebrate the 100th anniversary of Hill Auditorium's opening because of the building's central role in allowing UMS to become one of the premier presenters in the United States. It was on May 14, 1913, that the Chicago Symphony Orchestra under Frederick Stock opened Hill Auditorium at the 20th annual Ann Arbor May Festival, under UMS auspices. In the century that had elapsed since that inaugural, Hill had hosted most of the top names in classical music and witnessed some of their most notable performances. It became a widely loved performance venue in part because its acoustics are excellent in spite of its large size. So it was appropriate that the anniversary celebration kicked off in February with an open house featuring a Saturday morning physics lecture on the hall's acoustics. There were also tours of the entire facility led by me and U-M student bass player Charlie Reischl, who had educated himself about architect Albert Kahn.

The highlight of the anniversary celebration was the showing of a 57-minute documentary on 100 years of performances at Hill Auditorium. Titled *A Space for Music, A Seat for Everyone*, it was written, produced, and directed by Sophia Kruz, a talented U-M film graduate whom UMS had hired to create the documentary and other media. Later aired by Detroit Public Television, it received the Emmy for Best Historical Documentary at the State of Michigan Awards Ceremony. With all the monumental changes that had occurred at UMS during my tenure, and particularly our more recent adventurous programming, it felt grounding and settling to spend this time getting back in touch with our past and our legacies.

Notes

1. By 2009, Ben had left UMS to become the director of Northrop Auditorium at the University of Minnesota, a highly regarded presenting program. In 2016, Ben became director of performing arts for the City of Los Angeles Department of Cultural Affairs.

2. While Michael Boyd was unable to participate in the first creative residency, he came to the second in 2012 and with U-M faculty and students workshopped a production of *Boris Godunov*. Ralph later saw the play in a powerful production at Stratford-upon-Avon. Much credit for its success was given to the work done in Michigan during the creative residency.

3. In March 2009, the Frankels' lead gift to the University of Michigan Museum of Art had led to the opening of the 53,000-square-foot addition of the Maxine and Stuart Frankel and Frankel Family Wing.

eight
Winding Down and Moving On

The thought that it might be time to hang it up started entering my mind during the 2014–15 season. I absolutely loved what I was doing. I loved presenting the art that we put on the stage. I loved my UMS colleagues. I loved our audiences. I loved Ann Arbor. I was deeply engaged in my field at the national and international level and had colleagues and friends I cherished all over the world. But I had reached that milestone of age 70. You can't get there and not think about a new phase of life.

Looking in the mirror, I saw someone who was actually beginning to look older, and this forced me to think about the brevity of life. My father had died of cancer at age 69, and my older brother Jerry had recently died of lung cancer at 71. I wondered how much time I had left. If it was limited, I wanted to make sure I could spend a good part of it with Penny and with Matt, Renee, and our two grandsons Alex and Reid.

I also recognized that I could no longer offer UMS the same level of energy and dynamism that had always animated my career. When I took part in M-Team meetings, I had fewer fresh ideas and they didn't come quite as fast. At the same time, I noticed that the best ideas came from younger staff members. This seemed a sure sign that it was time to get out of the way for the next generation of leadership. I could still claim to have wisdom and experience, and that counted for something, but in the presenting business innovative thinking is key.

Then there was the practical issue of the work that fell onto my plate. Operational matters like revising the staff handbook, improving our office space, and designing a better performance review process demanded my attention and, though I recognized their critical importance, I frankly had very little interest in them. Maybe, I thought, somebody else ought to be worrying about these things. At the same time, the big-picture issues—particularly finance and budget—felt completely under control. UMS was receiving several significant multiyear grants from major foundations and we were partnering with U-M in the biggest fundraising campaign ever undertaken by a public university. Our present and future seemed secure.

The leader of an organization like UMS doesn't just step down—and I certainly wasn't ready to retire right away. A long period of transition is required. I knew I was looking at a retirement date a good two years into the future at least. But it was not too early to begin thinking about a date and what would need to happen in the intervening period. I began sharing these thoughts with my closest friends and colleagues.

One of those people was Michael Kondziolka. I was touched when Michael sat down with me midway through the 2014–15 season to talk about the season two years down the road. Speculating that 2016–17 might be my final season, Michael said that he would need a couple of years in advance to be able to assure that the artists I would like to see in that season would be able to be part of it.

We already knew that the Berlin Philharmonic would be coming for two performances in the middle of November in 2016, in what would be Sir Simon Rattle's final North American tour with the orchestra. That would be extra special. And we had to have Wynton Marsalis and his Jazz at Lincoln Center Orchestra back in the winter or spring of 2017, even though they were scheduled for an upcoming concert in February and another in early 2016. Wynton Marsalis and I had a special relationship. He had appeared in 16 seasons during my tenure. We had co-commissioned several of his works and hosted the world premiere of *A Fiddler's Tale*. He had invited me to speak to his Jazz at Lincoln Center board of directors in New York City after he and the ensemble received our 2014 Distinguished Artist Award.

Then there was Yo-Yo Ma. There's no other musician like him; he's just in a class by himself. Yo-Yo is the best at what he does, playing the cello, but he's never rested on his laurels. He is always exploring, collaborating with the most interesting artists, such as those who are part of his Silk Road Ensemble. And besides that he is just about the most wonderful human being imaginable. Michael and I talked about having him come in April 2017 with mandolin player Chris Thile and bassist Edgar Meyer to perform in the next-to-last concert of my UMS career.

Wynton Marsalis with Ken and Penny after Wynton and the Jazz at Lincoln Center Orchestra receive the UMS Distinguished Artist Award. March 30, 2014.

I told Michael that in my final year I'd love to have the King's Singers, the group that started it all for me with my presentation of them at the Kennedy Center Concert Hall on Valentine's Day 1983. That would bring my career full circle. They would perform in a holiday concert on December 10, 2016.

Soon after penciling in those highlights, we learned that the Takács Quartet, whom I had presented in 17 concerts during my tenure, was touring a complete cycle of the Beethoven string quartets during the 2016–17 season. We knew we had to book it. It would entail the quartet coming three times, for two concerts each visit in October, January, and March. Given these parameters, Michael and his team, Mark Jacobson and Liz Stover-Rosenthal, put together a magnificent final season for 2016–17.

In the meantime, there was plenty of heartwarming recognition and appreciation for what I had accomplished. In early March 2015, I received a message from Richard Kessler, the chair of Chamber Music America's board of directors, saying that I had been selected to receive CMA's Richard J. Bogomolny National Service Award. This honor meant a great deal to me, in part because of the high value I placed on chamber music and also because the award was named for a man for whom I had great admiration and respect (and had succeeded as chair of CMA). At the Awards Banquet ten months later, at the annual conference of Chamber Music America in New York in January 2016, chamber-musician members of my family performed. Aaron Dworkin, whom I had mentored beginning in the mid-1990s, was invited to interview me as part of the conference activities, and he put together a slide show about me. It was a very special occasion.

Then there was an even greater honor. In August 2015, I received a phone call from Jane Chu, chair of the National Endowment for the Arts. She had exciting news: UMS was one of the recipients of the 2014 National Medal of Arts. This award, the highest given to artists and arts patrons by the U.S. government, was very prestigious. For UMS, the distinction was amplified because we would be the first university-affiliated presenter to receive it. I was overcome with gratitude: receiving the medal as the leader of UMS would be a fitting cap to my career and an acknowledgment of how far we had taken the organization during my near-30 years as its president. Further, I was happy that it was an institutional award—a recognition of the contributions of my predecessors as well as those of our audience, board, staff, and volunteers, all the wonderful people who had supported UMS for so many years.

Jane congratulated UMS on being so recognized and invited me to the White House on September 10 to accept the award from President Obama on behalf of UMS. When I received the call, Penny and I were in Washington just as Penny was about to receive the National Flute Association's Distinguished Service Award for her more than 40 years of service to the field and to the association. Both of us felt very appreciated in similar ways that day.

Throughout the preliminary preparations for the White House event, which were ongoing for about a month following the August phone call, we kept trying to get the White House officials to refer to us by our official name: "University Musical Society of the University of Michigan." It was important that our official name be used because it's the University of Michigan that people would recognize. I knew this was especially true for the president and First Lady. President Obama received an honorary degree and was the speaker at the 2010 Spring Commencement at Michigan Stadium. He visited again in the spring of 2014, giving a speech at the Al Glick Field House. "University Musical Society" would mean very little to him, but "University of Michigan" was full of significance.

The official emails, however, kept referring to us only as "University Musical Society." I requested several times that they use our official name. There was no change. I finally received a listing of the other 10 recipients of the 2014 National Medal of Arts. I looked at how author Stephen King would be honored; there was no mention of any of his books or films. I looked at how Sally Field would be honored; there was no mention of any of her films. Oh, what the heck! I tried.

On the tenth of September, I was standing in line in the State Dining Room, preparing to be photographed with the Obamas in the Red Room, when I remembered that during the president's last visit on campus in 2014 he praised U-M basketball player Jordan Morgan during his remarks. That was the hook I needed. One of the ways of connecting with people is knowing what's important to them and using that knowledge to get them interested in what's important to you. The president was no exception.

When President Obama delivered his speech during his 2014 visit to Ann Arbor, Jordan Morgan was on his way to setting three school records in basketball—career games played (142), career field-goal percentage (63.1 percent), and single-season field-goal percentage (70 percent). Jordan had also been on the teams that played for the NCAA Championship in 2013 and won the regular season Big Ten Championship in 2014. He would graduate from Michigan a few months later with both a bachelor's and master's degree in engineering. The president had praised Jordan's basketball success but highlighted his academic achievements as well.

Significantly, I knew Jordan well. During his final year at Michigan, he accompanied me to performances at UMS as a member of the Order of Angell, meeting the actors and actresses I introduced to him after performances. He was soaking up as much art as possible before graduating, in part because his girlfriend, KT Maviglia, was a dance major. In the process, Jordan became an articulate spokesperson for the value of the arts in education.

While waiting to meet the president, I tried to contact Jordan in Italy, where he was playing professional basketball, but I couldn't reach him. It was then about one minute away from my being introduced to the president. A marine handed me a piece of paper with "University Musical Society" written on it and told me, "This is what you give to the marine inside

On September 10, 2015, President Barack Obama awarded UMS the 2014 National Medal of the Arts, the nation's highest public artistic honor, given to those who have "demonstrated a lifetime of creative excellence."

the Red Room, who will announce you to the president and First Lady." I said, "Thank you very much." As the gentleman passed, I took out my pen and added "of the University of Michigan" to the slip of paper. That's what I handed to the marine as I was about to be announced and said to him, "Read the whole thing."

There stood President and Mrs. Obama; the marine announced, "University Musical Society of the University of Michigan." The Obamas lit up as they heard the words "the University of Michigan." I went toward the president, he put out his hand, and I said, "Jordan Morgan says 'Hi.'" The President beamed. Then they had me stand between them for the photo. As the photographer was getting ready, the president said, "How's Harbaugh doing? Wish him well for me." Michelle said, 'Would you tell Jim Harbaugh how much I appreciate all the work he's doing for charities in Detroit?" I looked at both of them, and I said, "That's exactly what I'll do."

I didn't know Jim Harbaugh, the new head coach of the football team, but I did know his son James, an aspiring theater major at U-M. I had met James at the beginning of the year when I handed him a set of tickets to all of the theater events to be presented at the University during the 2015–16 season. These tickets were a high school graduation gift from Harbaugh family friends Todd and Terri Anson, who knew that James was a theater lover.

Two weeks after the White House ceremony, I was at the Brigham Young vs. Michigan football game with Priscilla Lindsay, the chair of the theater department. I had been hoping to be able to connect James Harbaugh Jr. with Priscilla, and knowing that James was likely at the game, I texted him to learn his whereabouts and see if he could rendezvous with us. James didn't respond to my several text messages during the game. I told Priscilla that I would connect her with James at another time.

After the game Penny and I were enjoying dinner at Knight's Steakhouse on Liberty with Carl Grapentine—the voice of Michigan Stadium—and his friend Kyle Dzapo, a flutist friend of his whom Penny and I also know. During dinner James called, apologizing for not having picked up the messages during the game. He invited us to come over to his father's home on Arlington Boulevard. As we were still eating dinner, I asked if we could come over later as I had some messages to deliver to his father. "That would be even better," he said. "All the coaches and recruits would be gone. It would just be my dad, my grandpa, and me and a few other family members." We headed to the Harbaugh home. James greeted us at the door. James's grandfather, Jack Harbaugh, and his father, Jim, were watching a game. They got up to meet us. I started off by saying, "Jim, the first thing I have to do is tell you what the President Obama and his wife wanted me to tell you when I was at the White House two weeks ago." I relayed the president's well wishes and the First Lady's praise and, of course, this elicited a big broad smile. Then Jim said, "Now remind me . . . who are you and why were you at the White House?"

Then was not the time to give him a little speech about UMS. "Jim, I'll get to that in a minute," I said. "What's important for you to know is that there are two Big Houses at the University of Michigan. There is your Big House, a vision of Fielding Yost who opened Michigan Stadium with 84,000 people in 1927. Now Jim, if Yost's vision had been any smaller, you wouldn't be where you are, Michigan wouldn't be a consistently high-ranked team, and Michigan wouldn't be the winningest football team

Ken with Jim, James, Jr., and Jack Harbaugh and with Carl Grapentine and Kayle
Dzapo at the Harbaugh home following the Brigham Young vs. U-M game. September 26, 2015.

in the country." Harbaugh nodded in acknowledgment. "The other Big
House," I went on, "is Hill Auditorium, the Big House for the arts, one of
the largest performing venues in the world with great acoustics. Had the
vision of Arthur Hill, Charles Sink, and Albert Kahn been any smaller, I
wouldn't be where I am, UMS wouldn't be bringing in the greatest musicians in the world to our community, and I wouldn't be going to the White
House to accept the National Medal of Arts." He nodded again. I could
tell he was seeing the connection. Then I said, "Next to Hill Auditorium is
Burton Memorial Tower, named after a great university president named

Marion Leroy Burton who died at age 50 after serving from 1920 to 1925. And on the top of that tower is one of the most distinguished collections of bells in the world, a carillon, a gift of the first athletics director of the University, Charles Baird. And do you know what else Baird did? He hired Fielding Yost." Harbaugh just beamed at us.

The next day, Chris Partridge, head of player personnel, wrote me an email message. "Hello Mr. Fischer, Coach Harbaugh mentioned that he met you recently and was very excited about everything going on at UMS. I would love to chat sometime about both our teams and what we can show recruits when they're in town. Let me know when you have some availability this week to talk briefly. Appreciate it! Have a Blessed Sunday!"

After exchanging a few emails, Chris and Erik Williams came over to experience the tower and Hill Auditorium. They saw the view, played the bells, and chatted with us about ideas. Then a few weeks later, in early November, I got a call from Jim Harbaugh. "Ken, I got an idea for something special on Signing Day." National Signing Day was when high school football players committed to the university where they wanted to play football. Then Harbaugh described how he wanted to create a memorable event. "I want Tom Brady here. I want Derek Jeter. I want my brother John here," he said. Jim envisioned the Hill stage with an ESPN-style broadcast table behind which Lou Holtz and other sports dignitaries would be sitting. There would be giant screens, produced videos, links to hometowns, and so on. "Don't tell a soul about this," said Harbaugh. "Can you help me get Hill Auditorium for this event?" I responded "Absolutely." I didn't tell Jim that I didn't control the scheduling of Hill Auditorium. Fact is, UMS pays rent to the University each time we use Hill Auditorium. Fortunately, the person who did schedule Hill, Shannon Rice, happened to be a big Michigan football and Jim Harbaugh fan. I told Shannon Rice of Jim's request, and she was able to make Hill available on February 3, the actual Signing Day, as well as the day before for the extensive set-up that would be required to meet Jim's goals.

It was a huge success. Hill was packed. The next day, on the front page of the *New York Times* sports section, there as an article on U-M's Signing Day with a large photo shot from the balcony showing a packed Hill Auditorium.

I went backstage afterward. Jim gave me a big hug and said, "Let's do it again. What can I do for you?" I reminded him that I had invited him and his wife, Sarah, to be the honorary chairs of UMS's spring benefit at

Crisler Arena in May. He accepted, and he and Sarah were a big hit with the UMS crowd.

During the spring and summer of 2015 I had talked about my retirement plans with a number of different people—Penny, U-M benefits folks, my financial adviser, board chair Stephen Forrest, some other board members, and key UMS staff colleagues. I considered all their input and decided that I would step down on June 30, 2017, the end of my 30th year at UMS. I communicated this formally to the board at its September 29 meeting. Announcing my plans at this time—21 months in advance—would give the board plenty of time to undertake a search for my successor. It was agreed that there would be no public announcement for a while. That would come after we had all our ducks in a row: a search committee and search firm identified, a proper set of statements from the board chair and me, a press release, and a set of talking points for board and staff.

I had accepted the National Medal of Arts on behalf of UMS at the White House only 19 days previously. I took the medal and the certificate to the board meeting to share with everyone, emphasizing how much it was a joint honor and appreciating the good relationship I'd enjoyed with the board during my 30-year tenure. Showing off the medal and announcing my retirement at the same time seemed wonderfully complementary; each gave more meaning to the other.

One board member, Mark Clague, a good friend and a professor of music who had led the effort to create the Gershwin Initiative at Michigan and who was instrumental in launching the EXCEL Lab (Excellence in Entrepreneurship, Career Empowerment & Leadership) came up to me after the meeting to invite me to teach a one-credit Arts Leadership mini-course through the EXCEL Lab beginning in the fall of 2017. I told Mark I was interested and saw his invitation as an indication of the kinds of connections I could maintain with the university after retirement.

In October, a few weeks after I made the announcement to the board, the New York Philharmonic came to Ann Arbor for a three-day residency made possible by a generous gift from U-M alumnus and UMS National Council member Eugene Grant, a real estate developer and philanthropist in New York City. The residency included three Hill Auditorium performances (one featuring Bernstein's score for *On the Waterfront* performed by the orchestra with the film projected on a large screen), master classes, miniperformances at University Hospital, and social functions. What

The New York Philharmonic performs at Hill Auditorium, October 10, 2015.

would be most widely remembered about the weekend, however, was a special event orchestrated by a member of our programming and production staff, Liz Stover Rosenthal. She saw an opportunity to include members of the New York Philharmonic brass section in the halftime celebration of the Northwestern vs. Michigan Homecoming game on October 10, 2015. Working with the U-M director of the Marching Band, John Pasquale, and officials at the New York Philharmonic, Liz helped produce a halftime show of classical music favorites that featured the brass of the NY Phil, the full Michigan Marching Band, the Alumni Band, the UMS Choral Union, and the flag crew, with NY Philharmonic music director Alan Gilbert conducting. There were nearly 1,000 participants in all. The NCAA rated it one of the top five half-time shows during the 2015 football season.

The day before the game, I arranged for the 97-year-old Gene Grant, his daughter Terry, and other members of their party to attend the rehearsal at Michigan Stadium. I introduced Gene to the 1,000 performers on the field and the several thousand spectators in the crowd. Gene gave a big wave to everyone as he was given hearty applause and cheers. He loved having a role in bringing *his* orchestra to *his* campus.[1]

The New York Philharmonic players, including principal clarinetist Anthony McGill, participated in master classes with U-M students during their October 2015 residency in Ann Arbor.

My guest for the game that day was Matthew VanBesien, president of the New York Philharmonic. As we walked with the Michigan Marching Band from Revelli Hall to Michigan Stadium, I mentioned confidentially to Matthew, given that we were planning future projects together, that I had told the UMS board a few weeks before that I would be hanging it up at UMS at the end of the 2016–17 season. He nodded and said he appreciated the heads-up.

In November, about a month after the New York Philharmonic residency, I was at Sundance in Utah with the National Arts Strategies board of directors and alumni from the organization's Chief Executive Program. One of the board members, Sally Sterling, was managing the nonprofit arm of Spencer Stuart, a leading executive search firm. I told Sally of my decision to step down from UMS and that the UMS board would be looking for a search firm to work with. Sally had managed the searches for a number of high-profile positions, such as the presidencies of the Ford Foundation,

The New York Philharmonic Brass join the Michigan Marching Band, Alumni Band, UMS Choral Union, and others performers during halftime of the Northwester vs. Michigan Homecoming Game at the Big House on October 10, 2015.

Kresge Foundation, Doris Duke Charitable Foundation, Wallace Foundation, New York Philharmonic, Chicago Symphony, National Public Radio, the Public Broadcasting System, and the Corporation for Public Broadcasting. Within less than a week, without my specifically inviting a proposal from her—it wasn't my role to do so—Sally sent me a full-fledged proposal. I shared it with the executive committee of the board as a sample of what I thought they should expect to receive and also suggested that they take a good look at Sally when the time came. After several months, they asked me to offer the names of other leading executive-search consultants in the nonprofit and art sectors, and I gave them the names of seven other firms. In the end, they selected Spencer Stuart and Sally Sterling to manage the search.

At the same time the board was looking into search firms, I was working with board chair Stephen Forrest on putting together a search committee. Again, it would not be my decision whom to select for the committee, but I appreciated the chance to weigh in on candidates. Steve and

Ken's team, all of whom started at UMS in the late 1980s and were with UMS when he retired in 2017 and whose combined service to UMS was 114 years: Clockwise (left to right) Ken, John Kennard, Michael Kondziolka, and Sara Billmann.

I agreed that the committee should include representatives from the UMS board and senate (former board members), the U-M faculty, the U-M administration, and the community. They should all be people engaged with UMS. I felt strongly that the committee also include someone from the UMS staff—with Michael Kondziolka, the longest-serving staff member, being the logical candidate. Finally, I thought the committee should include a university performing arts presenter who would not wish to be a candidate for the position but knew UMS and its stature in the field. For this slot I recommended Mike Ross, executive director of the Krannert Center at the University of Illinois at Urbana-Champaign. I was pleased that Steve Forrest accepted all my recommendations.

By April 7, a little over six months after I had told the board about my retirement, we had everything in place for the roll out of the public announcement. Sara Billmann, UMS director of marketing and communications, had prepared a press release (and sent it out embargoed until April 7). Sara had also prepared a briefing sheet for the board and staff that provided guidance on how to respond to the inevitable questions: Why are you announcing this now? Why is Ken choosing to retire next year? Has a search committee been named? When will a new leader be selected? What is UMS looking for in a new leader? Will there be an opportunity to celebrate Ken?

For my part, I wanted to let friends, colleagues, and other people in my network know about my decision to retire via a more personal note. I held my breath and hit the send button on the email, which was addressed to everyone on my contact list. My note expressed what a privilege it had been to have worked with so many talented and dedicated people over the years. I praised "the vibrant community of Ann Arbor," the University of Michigan, and our audience, which I noted was "the best-informed, most adventurous, and most passionate audience" our guest artists knew. I went on to explain the reasons behind my decision and to describe my excitement about the next generation of leadership. I wrote that UMS was in the best shape it had ever been and made it clear that the members of the board and staff were primarily responsible.

The official press release covered all the ground it would be expected to. I thought it did a particularly fine job summarizing how UMS had grown during the 29 years I served as its leader:

> Fischer . . . has overseen the organization's artistic growth and diversification into ongoing commitments to art forms outside of classical music; expansion into K-12, university, and community education programs; and initiatives to put UMS on a secure financial footing. Under Fischer's visionary leadership, UMS has greatly expanded and diversified its programming and its audiences, deepening its engagement with the University (including relationships with 70 academic units and more than 200 faculty) and southeast Michigan communities; created exemplary partnerships with leading artistic collaborators across the world; taken an active role in commissioning new works; and received significant grants awarded by prominent foundations that support the arts, including the Wallace Foundation, the Andrew W. Mellon Foundation, and the Doris Duke Charitable Foundation.

It was important to me that the press release noted that the "everybody in, nobody out" philosophy that I had learned from Patrick Hayes was "now intrinsic to UMS's work and guides the organization in building a truly inclusive and multicultural community around all its mainstage and educational programming." The press release concluded with a reassuring quote from me: "While I get a lot of the credit for UMS's success, I have a terrific team of over 30 colleagues that makes it all happen, and they will continue to do so after I retire as president."

A little more than a week after the public announcement of my retirement, UMS announced the lineup for the 2016–17 season, noting that it included "several concerts programmed with Ken's final year in mind."

From April 7 until the fall, I had nothing to do with the activities of the search committee or search firm. I never inquired about it; no one ever talked to me about it. That's the way I hoped it would work. I had great faith in the committee.

In June, after the end of the 2015–16 season, the compiled financial reports showed that we'd had the best year since I'd been president. We'd set a goal for our box office at the season's outset and exceeded it by 18 percent. We'd never had that high of an increase in ticket sales above our projected goal. Though I was thrilled with that result in itself, I found it truly amazing that we'd hit it at the ticket office even though we had moved into programming that was often challenging, provocative, and uncomfortable. That added to the feeling of accomplishment I had as I started my final year.

During the summer of 2016, while the search committee was doing its work, Penny and I celebrated our 50th wedding anniversary with a trip to Rome and a cruise that took us to various parts of Italy and Greece. Then we gathered with Matt's family at Camp Michigania, U-M's family alumni camp, for a week in August.

One of the most memorable and inspiring weekends of my entire time at UMS took place, fittingly, near the beginning of my final season. It coalesced around the pair of Berlin Philharmonic performances we had scheduled a couple of years earlier. The tone for the weekend was set when I drove the conductor, Sir Simon Rattle, to Ann Arbor from the nearby Willow Run Airport, where the orchestra's chartered jet had landed. During the ride, I told Sir Simon what a great privilege it was for us in Ann Arbor to be able to present the Berlin Philharmonic. He looked at me with a grin and chuckled. He explained that once he had been named the orchestra's conductor and it was time to plan the next North American tour, the orchestra members had made it very clear to him that a stop in Ann Arbor was a given. "We love coming to Ann Arbor!," he told me.

The two performances themselves, on November 12 and 13, were leap-to-your-feet amazing. But the weekend was packed with much more. Berlin Philharmonic principal players taught crowded master classes. Sir Simon led an extraordinary conducting seminar. My brother-in-law Bill Lutes gave an outstanding talk at the prelude dinner. A reception for all orchestra members featured a highly accessible and gracious Sir Simon. Students of all ages were everywhere thanks to free educational events and deeply discounted tickets; many Fischer family members and long-time friends came to town from all over the country. A crew from CBS's *60 Minutes* captured it all, filming for a special feature on the maestro that would be broadcast later. I was enormously proud of my amazing UMS colleagues, who pulled it off superbly.

A little more than a week later, right before Thanksgiving 2016, I received a call from search committee chair Steve Forrest. I was having lunch alone at Red Hawk on South State Street. Steve told me that the committee was going to bring a leading candidate to campus the week after Thanksgiving and that I would be expected to meet with the candidate along with other members of the UMS management team. Then Steve told me who it was: Matthew VanBesien. At first I couldn't believe it. Here was the president of the New York Philharmonic showing interest in the UMS gig. I was so excited that I told Steve to hang on for a moment, left the restaurant with the phone in my ear, ran down South State Street to East Liberty, turned left and found a seat outside the Michigan Theatre. Steve explained that Sally Sterling was not able to participate in Matthew's UMS recruitment because she had been the search consultant to the New York Philharmonic when they hired Matthew only five years before, and her ethical standards prevented her from 'poaching' someone she had previously placed. That means Matthew had expressed interest in the position on his own. The courting of Matthew became intense from that point on with UMS board members and staff and university officials all working together to win Matthew over.

Matthew decided to take the position right after the holidays in early January 2017. I couldn't have been happier. With the official announcement scheduled for Tuesday morning, January 24, at 10:15am in the *New*

President Schlissel, Matthew VanBesien, and Ken at NYC's Lincoln Center a few days before the official announcement of Matthew's succeeding Ken as UMS President. January 2017.

York Times, we had to keep this news in strictest confidence until then. Matthew and I met for brunch at French Roast on the Upper West Side on Sunday, January 15, while I was in the city for the annual presenters' conferences. I let him know how thrilled I was and how excited I knew the staff would be, since many of them had gotten to know him when he came out with the New York Philharmonic for their concert in 2013 and their residency in 2015. I let him know that I would be available to him if there was anything he needed, but that I would stay out of his way and let him be the president of UMS. We noted that we had four things in common: we were both Midwestern French horn players who had attended Interlochen Arts Camp and Big Ten universities.

A month after the announcement of Matthew's decision, Michael Kondziolka and I met with U-M president Mark Schlissel to give him a heads-up on four plays UMS would be presenting in January 2018. This was six months after I would have left, but the performances were being planned under my watch. These plays would be part of our first *No Safety*

Net theater series, a three-week festival embracing contemporary social issues through four different productions. They would deal with issues of slavery, terrorism, transgender identity, and radical wellness and healing. President Schlissel said that he welcomed such plays as a way of fostering timely conversations where all points of view would be welcomed. We assured him that UMS would present a suite of contextual programs, including workshops, lectures, panel discussions, and other activities intended to encourage open and constructive dialogue and to embrace the calls-to-action embedded in the theatrical presentations. Once this conversation wrapped up, I asked to speak with President Schlissel alone.

With Matthew having just accepted the position as UMS president, I asked Mark if he had any advice for me about how I might handle the leadership transition. I observed that he had succeeded a long-serving popular president, Mary Sue Coleman. He thought the transition had gone very well. She was always available if he needed her for anything, but she let him be the president of the University of Michigan. I had a sense before going in that the best way for me to behave was to stay out of Matthew's way, and the wisdom of that approach was reinforced by what Mark had to say.

It didn't hurt that I had absolute faith in Matthew's abilities. I was being succeeded by an outstanding leader who knew UMS and was genuinely excited about venturing into the world of multidisciplinary presenting. Plus, Matthew was my friend and I wanted what was best for him. I knew that the last thing he needed was the "old guy" hanging around.

I would still be going to UMS concerts and other performances, however—UMS would graciously provide Penny and me with a pair of tickets to regularly scheduled UMS concerts into the future—and this raised similar issues. I didn't want seating that would put us "in the way" of the pre- and postperformance "schmoozing" that the president of UMS would naturally want to do. I made this clear to the members of the board and staff, and they agreed. We also created an understanding that I would refrain from going backstage after a concert without gaining permission from Matthew or the lead staff person for the event. We have a very crowded backstage situation at UMS and no easy access from where the head of the organization would sit. When the president of the organization wants to host the concert sponsor in a meet-and-greet with the guest artists at U-M auditoria, it needs to be orchestrated in advance because it's complicated. With getting the donor to the artist as the top priority, the

The Fischer family at Revelli Hall. Alex and Reid in front. Matt, Penny, Ken, Renee behind. November 5, 2016

president doesn't want to worry about the "old guy" worming his way in because he feels entitled. It felt good to iron out these rules of engagement ahead of time.

My wonderful colleagues at UMS designed two "official" retirement events that touched me deeply. The first was held on May 6, 2017 at Crisler Center. I was kept in the dark about the specifics of the evening other than that I should show up in a tux with Penny and just enjoy the evening. I knew that family was coming in from around the country but didn't know what role, if any, they would have in the evening's festivities. My dear colleague Colleen Jennings-Roggensack flew in from Tempe, Arizona, and served as comaster of ceremonies with former UMS intern and U-M musical theater alum Leonard Navarro. There was a printed program, but I chose just to let the evening unfold in front of me.

 Highlights included performances by the UMS Choral Union, two principal dancers from the Martha Graham Company, family members from both the Peterson and Fischer sides, dear friends Bill Bolcom and

The Michigan Marching Band spells out "Fischer" at the Big House on the day the UMS Board of Directors sponsored the halftime show during Ken's last year with UMS. November 5, 2016.

Joan Morris, and Carla Dirlikov Canales and Christina Maxwell, two remarkably talented women I met when they were students. Steven Jarvi retold the story of "Claudio Abbado and the Cigar" and conducted a student ensemble playing "The Victors" and other pieces. U-M president Mark Schlissel had some kind words to say, and I was touched that our congresswoman, Debbie Dingell, attended. I circulated throughout the floor of the Crisler Arena—Michigan's basketball court—and greeted as many of the 700 guests as I could. As the evening was winding down, Dave Barrett came to the piano and played the four-minute "Golden Street" prelude to his iconic sports song "One Shining Moment." Then attention turned to the screen, where a highlight video of my career at UMS ran to a recording of "One Shining Moment."

Many dear colleagues and friends—Ruth Felt, Jackie Davis, Ted and Teresa Marchese, Charlie Hamlen, Elisabeth Hayes, Barbara Fleischman, David Baile, Mike Ross, Sally Sterling, and Jan Kallish—made a special effort to be there. Maria Claudia Parias came all the way from Bogota, Columbia. I felt a special spot in my heart that night for Emmy Lewis, who flew in from Washington, D.C., for the event. It was Emmy who called me from Lois Stegeman's kitchen in the summer of 1986 and told me, "Get your resume in here by Monday! Your next job is here in Ann Arbor."

A second retirement party came three weeks later on June 1, 2017—30 years to the day from when I started at UMS. It was a "y'all come" event, free and open to the entire community. And what else could it be called but "Everybody In, Nobody Out"? It was held in the Assembly Room on the 4th floor of the Rackham Building. There I received the key to the city and proclamations from Ann Arbor mayor Christopher Taylor and other proclamations arranged by Congresswoman Debbie Dingell, Governor Rick Snyder, and the Michigan House of Representatives. I was especially touched when a group of members from Local 395 of the International Alliance of Theatrical Stage Employees, the stagehands' union, presented me with a lifetime membership card. In my remarks I acknowledged three special people in attendance, all in their 90s, who played a critical role in my coming to UMS: John Reed, the emeritus law professor and Baptist church choir director who chaired the search committee that recommended me to the board in 1986, and Ginny and Bill McKeachie, who had known me from my U-M grad school days in the late 1960s and vouched for me with John Reed.

The last board meeting of my career came on Tuesday, June 27, 2017, three days before my official retirement date. Board chair Steve Forrest presented me with four gifts on behalf of the board: a beautiful Shinola Argonite 715 watch made in Detroit; a certificate for a 10-day cruise on the Great Lakes for Penny and me, arranged by Conlin Travel president and UMS board member Chris Conlin; an office in the College of Literature, Science, and Arts, courtesy of LSA dean Andrew Martin; and that most cherished of campus amenities, access to a special parking permit. I knew that both the office and the parking perk had required a great deal of wrangling and negotiating by board chair Steve Forrest, and I appreciated both immensely.

On Matthew VanBesien's first day on the job—July 3, 2017—I stopped by to give him my keys to the Burton Tower offices, my access card to the Liberty Street offices, and my UMS gold parking pass. I wished him well.

I left the office with a very good feeling. I was passing on the leadership of UMS to someone I had known for six years, with whom I'd created the 2015 New York Philharmonic residency. National Arts Strategies had identified Matthew for its prestigious Chief Executive Program; I knew he recognized the high-quality staff he would be inheriting. And, heck, he was a fellow horn player from the Midwest who had gone to Interlochen. What more could I want? That he was just a few years younger than I was when I became president of UMS gave me hope that he might be around for a while.

It's impossible to hand over the reins to an organization as big and important and venerable as UMS and not see your career in terms of legacies and the passing on of timeless values. I'm grateful to Mom and Dad for instilling in me the values that would guide my life and for providing the opportunities that led to my deep love for music and all the arts. My older brother Jerry was my best friend and trailblazer, and my younger siblings Norman and Martha deepened my love for music through their own boundless passion and talent as performers, teachers, and coaches. Penny, my companion for over 50 years, has been a constant inspiration in music and life, and together we brought Matt into the world and raised one magnificent young man. What a joy he, his wife Renee, and sons Alex and Reid have been for us.

I'd been fortunate to stand on the shoulders of my immediate predecessors at UMS Charles Sink and Gail Rector. And I'd been shaped by three remarkable men whose ideas formed much of who I am. Charlie McWhorter's enthusiasm for connecting people of different backgrounds and Bill Coffin's advocacy for taking actions based on moral convictions strongly influenced me, eventually merging with lessons from my mentor Patrick Hayes, whose vision of the arts as ultimate unifier was the greatest gift of all.

Because of the importance Hayes placed on it, collaboration became for me both the means to the end and an end itself. That's what "Everybody In, Nobody Out" meant in application. Much like Bo Schembechler, the great Michigan football coach, I advocated that it was all about "the team the team the team." That's really the foundation of UMS's success. We drew in remarkable people, we worked together as a team, we grew as a group, we respected the special talents that people brought in. Working from this core, everybody at UMS was committed to engaging with the community and to taking chances in a variety of ways—chances with culture, chances with people, chances with different kinds of art forms.

I had to recognize also that none of the last thirty years' achievements would have been possible without the remarkable community of Ann Arbor. I couldn't allow myself to forget it takes an audience that is willing to show up, willing to be challenged at times, and taken out of their comfort zone every once and a while. And I knew that Ann Arbor had these characteristics because it was the home of a great university. I felt tremendously fortunate to have as UMS's closest partner the University of Michigan, an institution with a deep history and a commitment to serve the people of Michigan and the world.

After retirement, my life didn't change radically. I still had my ties to the university, an office in the LSA Building and later in the Residential College, and my friendships with professors, administrators, and UMS staff members. I was still involved with organizations serving the community, the field of arts presenting, education, and the arts generally.

In addition, I still had some limited involvement with UMS events. As part of the May 6 retirement celebration, colleagues had set up the Ken Fischer Legacy Endowment and requested that all attendees make a donation to the fund. Interest generated by the fund would support a UMS concert each year and related education and community engagement activities. Penny and I were invited to select which performance that would be. In the 2017–18 season we chose to apply the endowment to the recital by Emanuel Pahud, principal flute of the Berlin Philharmonic, and pianist Alessio Bax, in recognition of Penny's flute career. For the 2018–19 season we chose the residency of the Martha Graham Dance Company, in recognition of the 25th anniversary of the Martha Graham Centenary Festival of 1994. In the 2019–20 season the fund would support a recital by flutist James Galway, a longtime friend and for whose 60th birthday tour Penny wrote the program notes.

Friends who had retired cautioned me about accepting any new assignments right away. They urged me to "give it a year." I flouted this advice more than once. I signed on to teach a one-credit minicourse on Arts Leadership at the School of Music, Theatre & Dance in the fall term of 2017 (and again in the winter terms of 2019 and 2020). Then at the beginning of 2018, when the King's Singers launched a yearlong celebration of their 50th anniversary with a keen eye on their next 50 years, they invited me to become the volunteer president of their new King's Singers Global Foundation, which was devoted to furthering the aims of teaching, cultural collaboration, and social unity. How could I say no to the guys whose concert 35 years before at the Kennedy Center helped convince me to become a professional performing arts presenter?

In 2018, Ismael Ahmed, who opened my eyes to the Arab world beginning in 1995 and who had become a wonderful friend and partner to UMS and to me personally, invited me to become chair of a new Concert of Colors Advisory Board that he and I would put together. Ismael had founded the annual Concert of Colors, Metro Detroit's Annual Diversity Festival, nearly three decades ago. Its mission is "to bring together the diverse peoples of Southeast Michigan to share their cultures, music, and traditions in an atmosphere of celebration, respect and acceptance." The aim of the advisory board would be to aid Concert of Colors in bringing financial and long-term leadership stability to the organization, allowing it to be successful for another three decades. Again, I couldn't say no to a good friend who had been so important to me and to UMS.

In June 2019, Penny and I took advantage of our long-standing roles as hosts of overseas alumni tours with the U-M Alumni Association. In this capacity, we had done trips to Scandinavia, the British Isles, continental Europe, Russia, Africa, and Costa Rica. I could now embrace this "duty" with even more enthusiasm. We hosted the U-M alumni delegation on the Big Ten Mediterranean Marvels Cruise, for which our 28 U-M alumni joined over 300 alumni from the other 13 Big Ten universities.

During my career I received a variety of honors and awards, all of which I greatly appreciated and felt humbled by. But in early October 2019 I learned of another honor that meant more to me, personally, than any other: at the winter commencement ceremonies I would receive an honorary doctor of fine arts degree from the University of Michigan. The email from President Mark Schlissel was quite brief, noting that my "distinguished service" had "enriched not just the university, but Ann Arbor, all of southeast Michigan, and beyond," but when I read it to Penny and Matt I couldn't get to the end because I got so choked up. I'd recommended many others for honorary degrees but never imagined that I'd be deemed worthy of receiving one myself. I hadn't finished my earned doctorate at U-M because of getting involved so deeply in the arts, but here was the university where I had the unfinished business of the incomplete degree affirming that in pursuing that arts career to the best of my ability I had fulfilled the requirements in alternative and much more meaningful ways.

Note

1. Gene died on April 3, 2018. This sentence appeared in his obituary: "A high point in his long life was bringing the New York Philharmonic to the University of Michigan, where it played the *Ode to Joy* with the UM marching band in the 'Big House.'"

Acknowledgments

An incredible number of people contributed both to my ability to write this book and to the events described within it. The list below is far from exhaustive, and my sincere thank you to everyone whom I am unable to mention here but nevertheless helped make this project possible. It would be impossible to acknowledge the literally thousands of artists, donors, and audience members who have touched my life during my career. To these individuals, respectively, I am grateful for the remarkable art you brought to our stages and classrooms, for your generous gifts that made bringing the art to our community possible, and for your attendance that made it all worthwhile.

My parents: I thank my late parents, Beth Buckley Fischer (1916–2012) and Gerald John Fischer (1917–1987), for their love, support, and commitment to education and the arts in the lives of their children. I also thank them for showing me the values of gratitude, kindness, integrity, listening, respect, service, generosity, faith, and love.

My siblings: I was lucky to be one of four kids in our family and to have great relationships with my siblings. Jerry, older than I by 18 months, was my best friend and trailblazer. An outstanding student, talented musician, and natural leader who had successful careers in business and philanthropy, Jerry was the thoughtful, responsible, steady, and confident older brother. When it came to choosing Interlochen, Wooster, a college major, and presenting professional concerts, Jerry took the plunge first, and I made the same choices a year later. He died in 2015, and I miss him greatly. I remain close to my younger siblings, both professional musicians who perform and teach: Norman, a cellist and chamber musician, and Martha, a collaborative pianist. Each of my siblings married incredible spouses. Jerry married Cathie Long Fischer; Norman, Jeanne Kierman Fischer; and Martha, Bill Lutes. All have amazing children and grandchildren, too many to mention here, but they all know Uncle Ken loves them.

My own family: My wife, Penny, and son, Matt, played a key role in my becoming a professional arts presenter with their suggestion at a family council meeting in 1986 that I bring more stability and security to our home and find "a real job." Shortly thereafter, the UMS job opened up, and, well, I got that "real job." But there's so much more to be grateful for: Penny has known me 80% of my life, providing support and love for most of what is chronicled in this book. Matt's birth brought immense joy to us both. Matt and I formed a special bond that continues to this day, and we now have a wonderful daughter-in-law, Renee, and awesome grandsons, Alex and Reid, in our family.

Tom and Debby McMullen: Thank you to Tom and Debby McMullen for their encouragement and support from the moment I started thinking about writing a book. Their gift to UMS to support the project assures that proceeds from the book will benefit UMS directly. That pleases me greatly since giving back to UMS was a prime motivator from this project's beginning.

Publisher and Editors: I am grateful to the University of Michigan Press, including Director Charles Watkinson and Editorial Director Mary Francis for their decision to publish the book as well as to Mary, Scott Ham, Danielle Coty-Fattal, and Marcia LaBrenz, whose collective editorial efforts brought me from the beginning to the end of the process. To have U-M Press publish the book is deeply meaningful given my 63-year relationship with the University of Michigan, starting at age 12 with French horn lessons at U-M's Harris Hall. I am immensely grateful to Robin Lea Pyle, who helped me create the early drafts and overall organization; without her help I never would have begun the process. Finally, a big thank you to developmental editor Eric Engles, who did a remarkable job with the entire manuscript, assisting me with narrative, structure, and focus and helping me pull everything together for the final draft.

Reviewers: I am grateful to Sara Billmann, Susie Craig, Judith Hurtig, and an anonymous reviewer for their helpful edits and suggestions on the preliminary drafts, and to the 25 reviewers of the final manuscript for contributing their comments about the book. Thanks to David Smith and Peter Smith, the two primary photographers engaged by UMS during my tenure, who contributed most of the UMS event images that appear in this book, and to the Michigan Marching Band for the photos at Michigan Stadium. Thanks also to Mark Jacobson of the UMS staff for his help in researching the photos in the UMS archives.

UMS Staff and Management Team: I was blessed at UMS to work with people who had a passion for the arts, expertise in their respective areas, a collaborative spirit, and a deep commitment to serve the UMS family. We built on the strength of the UMS that preceded us and took the organization to a new level worthy of receiving the National Medal of Arts in 2015, the first university presenter to be so recognized. I wish I could thank each staff member and intern individually who served UMS during my 30 years, but that is not possible. I do want to recognize the UMS Management Team who as a group made the key decisions that guided UMS during my tenure. I give special thanks to three cherished colleagues whom I welcomed to UMS in the late 1980s and who were still with me on the day I retired: Michael Kondziolka, Sara Billmann, and John Kennard.

UMS Board of Directors and National Council: As the president of a nonprofit organization, I reported to a volunteer board of directors that met five to seven times a year and served a volunteer national council that met three times a year. I thank each volunteer for their dedicated service to UMS. We maintained exemplary board-staff relationships due to the quality of leadership in each board chair with whom I partnered. Unable to acknowledge each, I do want to recognize my first chair, John Reed; my last chair, Steve Forrest; my longest serving chair, Bev Geltner; and chair Clayton Wilhite, who was also the founding chair of the UMS National Council.

UMS Advisory Committee/Ambassadors: During my tenure, the group of UMS volunteers known as the Advisory Committee (later the Ambassadors) identified new ways to serve UMS, mainly through human and financial support to our education and community engagement program. They served as ushers for our school-day performances; raised funds through their *Bravo!* cookbook, On the Road auctions, and 20 Ford Honors Program dinners; assisted in each major artist residency transporting and hosting artists; provided support to UMS staff; and contributed so much more in other ways. My thanks goes to each Advisory/Ambassador chair and to all the members whose outstanding contributions to UMS are documented in *Together: A History of the UMS Advisory Committee and Ambassadors 1972–2017.*

UMS Choral Union: In 1879, four Ann Arbor church choirs joined together to perform choruses from Handel's *Messiah* in what became UMS's first concert on December 16. The UMS Choral Union remains a critical component of UMS as it brings town and gown together in a Grammy Award–winning volunteer chorus for memorable performances each year. I'm grateful to each member of the UMS Choral Union, to longtime manager Kathleen Operhall, and to each of the five conductors who served during my tenure: Donald Bryant, Thomas Hilbish, Thomas Sheets, Jerry Blackstone, and Scott Hanoian. One of the initiatives of the UMS Choral Union is the popular Summer Sings, the three evenings of choral reading sessions held each summer open to anyone who wishes to sing. While launched by conductor Thomas Sheets in 1994, the key reason it has succeeded is the dedicated volunteer who has overseen it from the very beginning, the indomitable Marilyn Meeker. Summer Sings continues to thrive because of Marilyn and her remarkable team. Thank you!

Interlochen Center for the Arts: The Interlochen Center for the Arts has been one of the most important institutions in my life, both during my youth and now as I remain involved as an alumnus, parent, and trustee. There are so many people connected to Interlochen—campers, counselors, teachers, staff, conductors, administrations, and fellow parents and alumni—who I wish I could acknowledge individually but that it is not possible here. I will always be grateful to Dr. Joseph E. Maddy, who founded Interlochen in 1928, and I look forward to celebrating its centenary in 2028. I thank my oldest and dearest friends of over 65 years—Mike Bresler, Lee Cabutti, Dave Posen, and Ron Stowe—and I thank Interlochen for bringing Charlie McWhorter and Penny into my life 60 years ago.

Washington Years: It was in Washington between 1970-87 where I gained valuable experience in both higher education and concert management, preparing me for UMS. Thanks to my colleagues at the American Association for Higher Education, Institute for Educational Leadership,

Levine School of Music, Music at Noon, and Washington Bach Consort, for everything I gained from each organization. Heartfelt thanks for their special friendship and contributions to my life to Russell Edgerton, John Merrow, Ted Marchese, and impresario Patrick Hayes, whose inclusion policy is the title of this book.

Ann Arbor—Landing the job and getting started: I'm grateful to the people who played a key role in my being appointed to the UMS job: Emmy Lewis, Jon McBride, Bill and Ginny McKeachie, John Reed, and Lois Stegeman as well as to those in the community who welcomed me warmly to Ann Arbor during a challenging first three months on the job: Jean Campbell, Sally and Robben Fleming, Bea and Bob Kahn, Rhea and Leslie Kish, Marjorie Lansing, Jerry and Judie Lax, and Phyllis Wright.

University of Michigan Faculty and Administrators: UMS built valued relationships with scores of partners during my years at the organization. I am extremely grateful to our closest partner, the University of Michigan, and the faculty and administrators spread throughout the campus who offered outstanding contributions. I offer special thanks to these faculty and administrators for being extraordinary partners throughout nearly my entire tenure at Michigan: Mark Clague, Erika Hrabec, Jeffrey Kuras, Catherine Lilly, Lester Monts, Marysia Ostafin, Birgit Rieck, Jim Toy, and Ralph Williams.

Cherished international colleagues: My life has been greatly enriched by colleagues from around the world who not only opened my mind and heart to their respective cultures but also became close friends. Thanks to each of you. I offer my deepest gratitude to the following individuals with whom I've shared special friendships spanning at least two decades: Bertha Cea, Robert Gilder, Maria Hansen, Eckard Heintz, Cristina King, Maria Claudia Parias, Benson Puah, Anthony Sargent, and Claudia Toni.

U.S. Artists Managers, Agents, Producers, and Consultants: I worked with many artist managers, agents, producers, and consultants over the years whose partnership led to memorable performances, outstanding educational programs, organizational improvements, and significant friendships. I wish I could thank each of them here. I do wish to recognize these significant partners whose friendship spans most of my career: Lisa

Booth, Alan Brown, Linda Brumbach, David Eden, Tim Fox, John Gingrich, Barbara Groves, Charles Hamlen, Steve Judson, Edna Landau, David Lieberman, Jack Mastroianni, Alice and Halsey North, Frank Salomon, Steve Shaiman, Douglas Sheldon, Sally Sterling, Nancy Wellman, and Tom Wolf.

U.S. arts presenting colleagues and arts association leaders. I wish to pay tribute to all of my U.S. performing arts presenting colleagues and arts association leaders who continue to teach and inspire me. I am especially grateful to three of my closest colleagues and founding partners of the Major University Presenters Network (MUPs): Colleen Jennings-Roggensack, Mike Ross, and Jerry Yoshitomi; to four who provided invaluable advice as I was just starting out and who remain close friends: Jackie Davis, Susie Farr, Ruth Felt, and Mikki Shepard; to six whose gifts of intellect, creativity, communication, and humanity have inspired me and countless others: Ben Cameron, Adrian Ellis, Diane Ragsdale, Neill Archer Roan, John Steinmetz, and Russell Willis Taylor; and finally to the association leaders with whom I worked most closely: David Baile, Richard Bogomolny, David Bury, Gail Crider, Mario Garcia Durham, David Fraher, Mark Resnick, and Dean Stein.

Southeast Michigan Arts, Education, Community, and Corporate Partners: "Getting out of the tower" and into the communities of Southeast Michigan enabled UMS to build significant partnerships with many sister arts organizations, educational institutions, nonprofit social service agencies, local businesses, and communities of shared heritage. The organizations and their representatives are too numerous to mention by name here, but I want each to know how much their partnership meant and how our work together enriched the lives of thousands throughout the region.

Private and Community Foundations: Support from the foundation community locally, regionally, and nationally was critical for UMS's advancing in the three areas of presentation, education, and creation. Heartfelt thanks to these foundation leaders for their long-term support of UMS and for their friendship over the years: Alberta Arthurs, Ben Cameron, Cheryl Elliott, Olga Garay English, Susan Feder, Neel Hajra, Ed Henry, Cheryl Ikemiya, Rory MacPherson, Mariam Noland, Mikki Shepard, Holly Sidford, Mariet Westermann, and Daniel Windham.

Media: I want to acknowledge my long-standing and valued relationship with the media and express my appreciation to these individuals for their commitment to meaningful arts coverage: Robert Aubry Davis, Susan Elliott, David Fair, Patricia Garcia, John Hilton, Rich Homberg, Jenn McKee, Molly Motherwell, Alberto Nacif, Susan Isaacs Nisbett, Steve Schram, Mark Stryker, Dave Wagner, Sherri Welch, and Linda Yohn.

Mentees: I have been fortunate to advise and mentor students, young professionals, and emerging leaders throughout my career. It is the joy of my life, especially as I'm now retired, to keep in touch and see how I might be helpful. More often than not these days, it is they who inspire me by the contributions they are making to their respective fields and to society. I wish I could name each of them, but I mention here those I have mentored who I know are now mentoring others: Josh Buoy, Carla Dirlikov Canales, Aaron Dworkin, Afa Sadykhly Dworkin, Erika Floreska, Xiang Gao, Maija Garcia, Chris Genteel, Heather Gladstein, Adam Glaser, Anna Glass, Maria Hansen, Steven Jarvi, Emil Kang, Heather Kendrick, Christina Maxwell, Michael Michelon, Jordan Morgan, Beth Morrison, Leonard Navarro, Paola Prestini, Claire Rice, Omari Rush, Phil Schermer, Marna Seltzer, Michael Steelman, Terri Trotter, KT Maviglia-Morgan, and Warren Williams.

My Men's Group: A decade ago I joined a group of guys who meet once a month. I am so grateful for their encouragement, insight, and humor over the past five years as I dealt with retirement and wrote this book. Thank you Steve Angerman, Frank Ascione, Bill Brinkerhoff, Paul Freedman, Bob Guenzel, Jeff Holden, Marvin Parnes, and our convener Rob Pasick.

Wynton Marsalis: I am deeply grateful to Wynton Marsalis, honorary chair of the UMS National Council, for writing the foreword. I was honored to present Wynton 19 times during my tenure at UMS, enabling my family and me, along with thousands in our community, to build a strong bond with this extraordinarily talented musician, composer, writer, speaker, humanitarian, and educator. My fondest memories are of Wynton the educator, whether it be his performing and speaking at a school-day performance at Hill, holding court with U-M jazz students till the wee hours at the Blue Nile, hanging out with the talented kids from Neutral Zone, or giving an impromptu lesson to two beginning elementary-school trumpet students back in his dressing room after they waited a hour to see him outside the stage door.

Matthew VanBesien: Finally, I thank my good friend Matthew VanBesien. I was thrilled when he succeeded me in July 2017, having known and worked with him since 2011, and I'm confident that UMS is in capable hands going forward. Thank you and continued best wishes, Matthew.

Index

Page numbers in bold represent photos.